# THE GIFT

The Gift
© Zoe Maeve Jenkins, 2021

First Edition
Printed by Gauvin Press in Gatineau, Quebec,
Canada

Library and Archives Canada Cataloguing
in Publication

Title: The gift / Zoe Maeve.
Names: Maeve, Zoe, author, artist.
Identifiers: Canadiana 2020038743X /
  ISBN 9781772620559 (softcover)
Subjects: LCSH: Anastasia Nikolaevna, Grand
  Dutchess, daughter of Nicholas II, Emperor
  of Russia, 1901-1918 — Comic books, strips,
  etc. / LCGFT: Historical comics. / LCGFT:
  Historical fiction. / LCGFT: Horror comics.
Classification: LCC PN6733.M34 G54 2021 /
  DDC 741.5/971—dc23

Conundrum Press
Wolfville, NS
www.conundrumpress.com

Distributed in Canada by Litdistco
Distributed in the US by Consortium
Distributed Internationally and in the UK
by Ingram

Conundrum Press acknowledges the financial
support of the Canada Council for the Arts,
the Government of Canada, and the
Province of Nova Scotia toward our
publishing program.

# Tsarskoye Selo, Russia, 1901

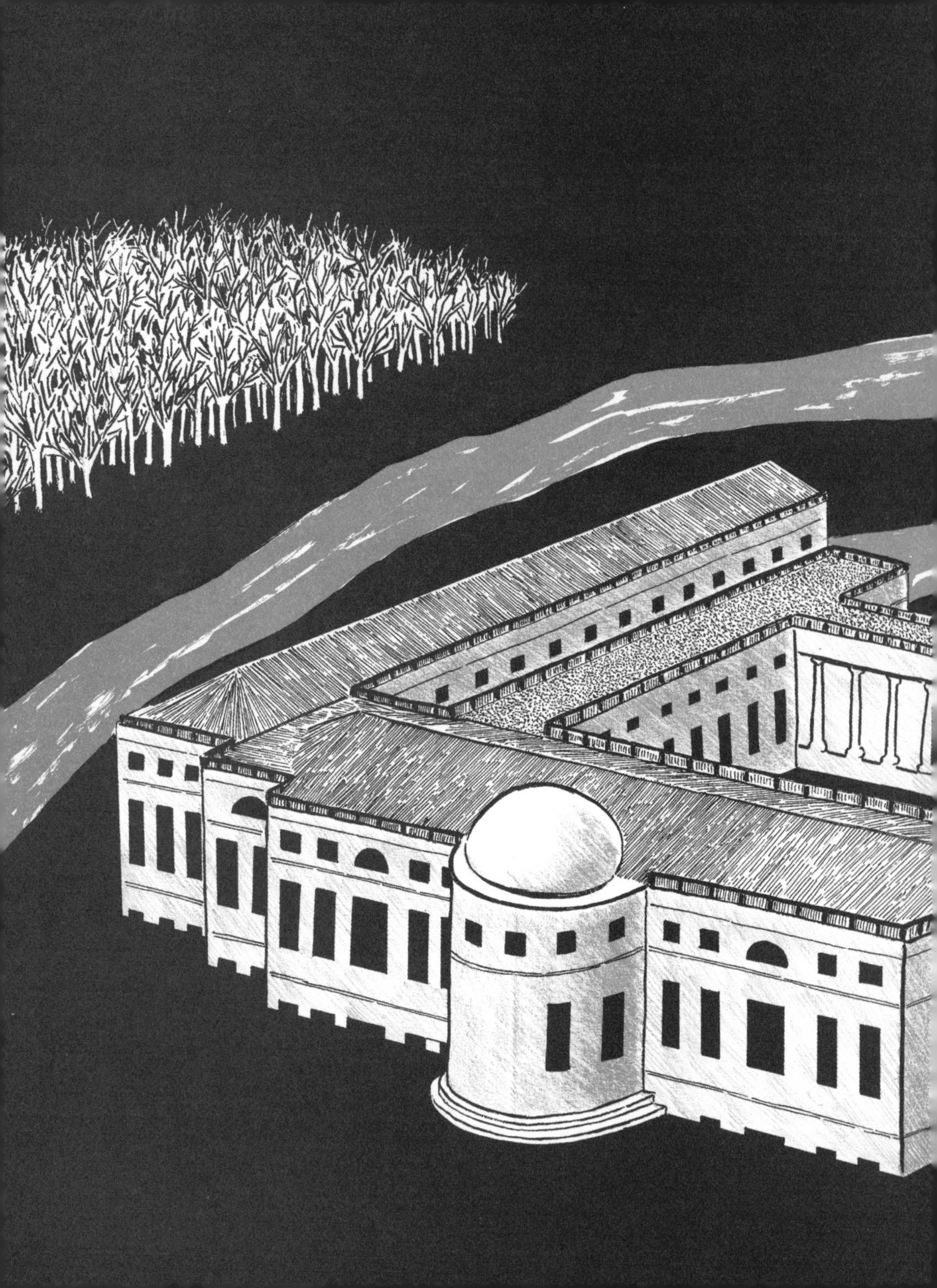

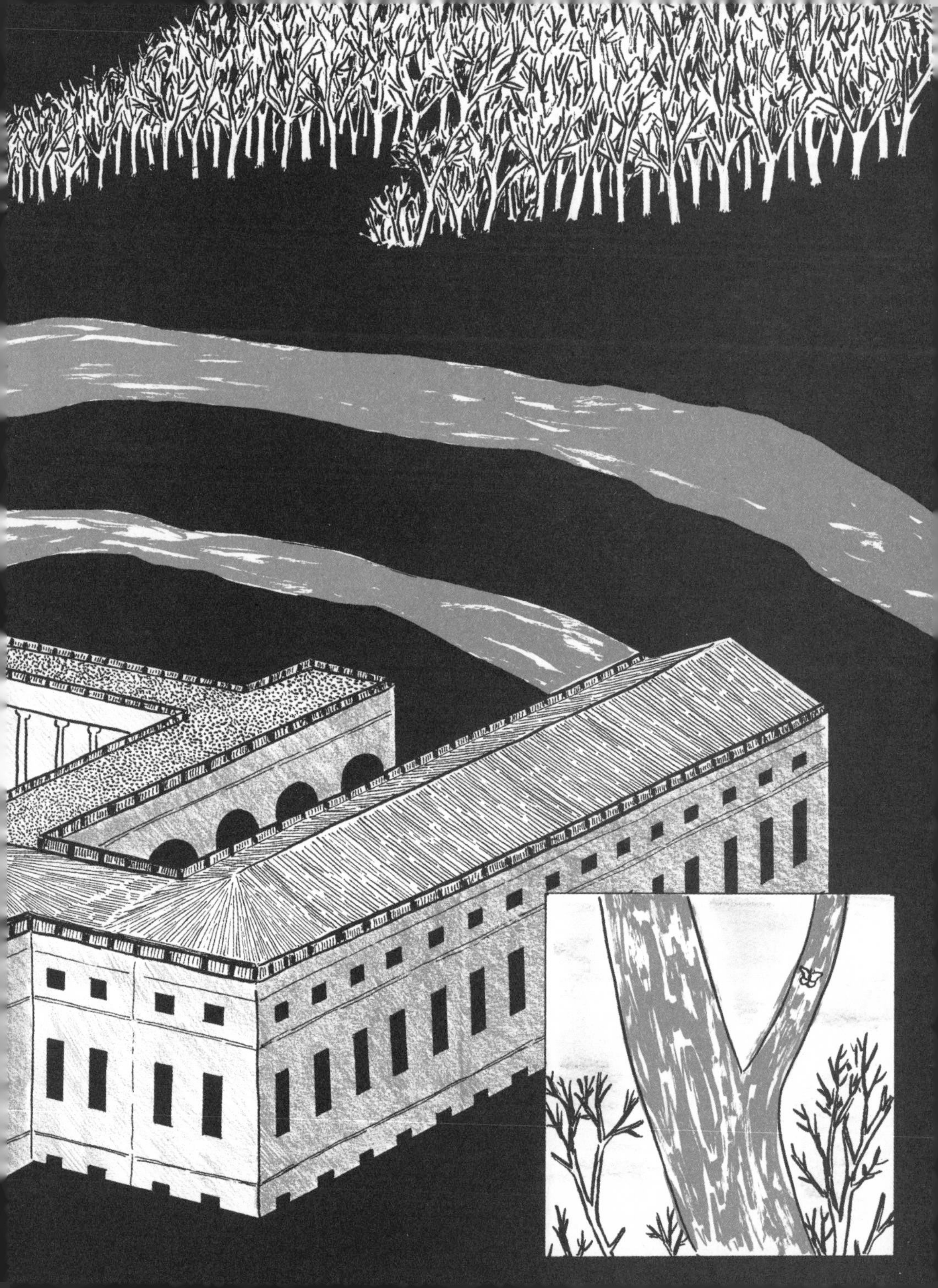

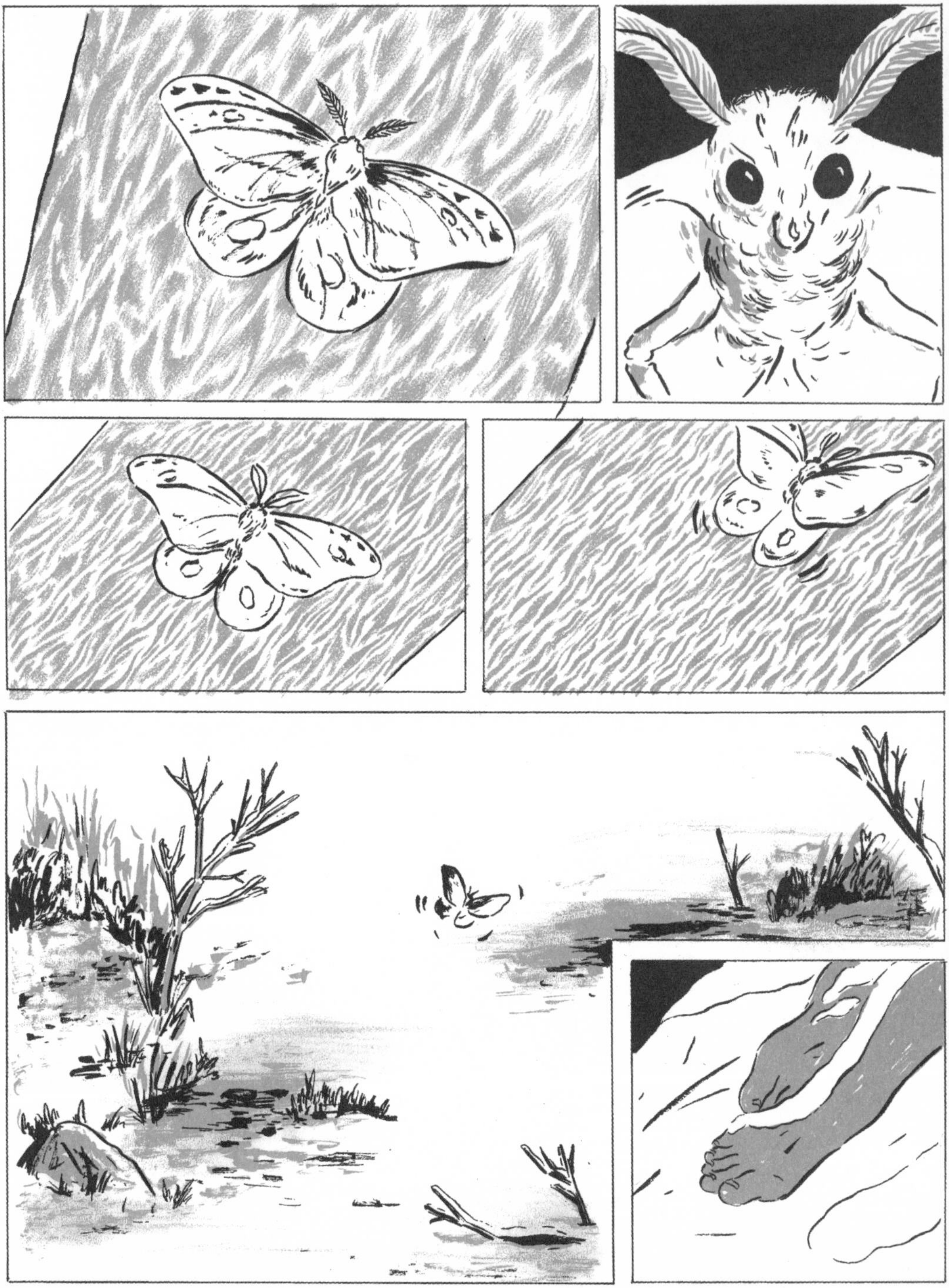

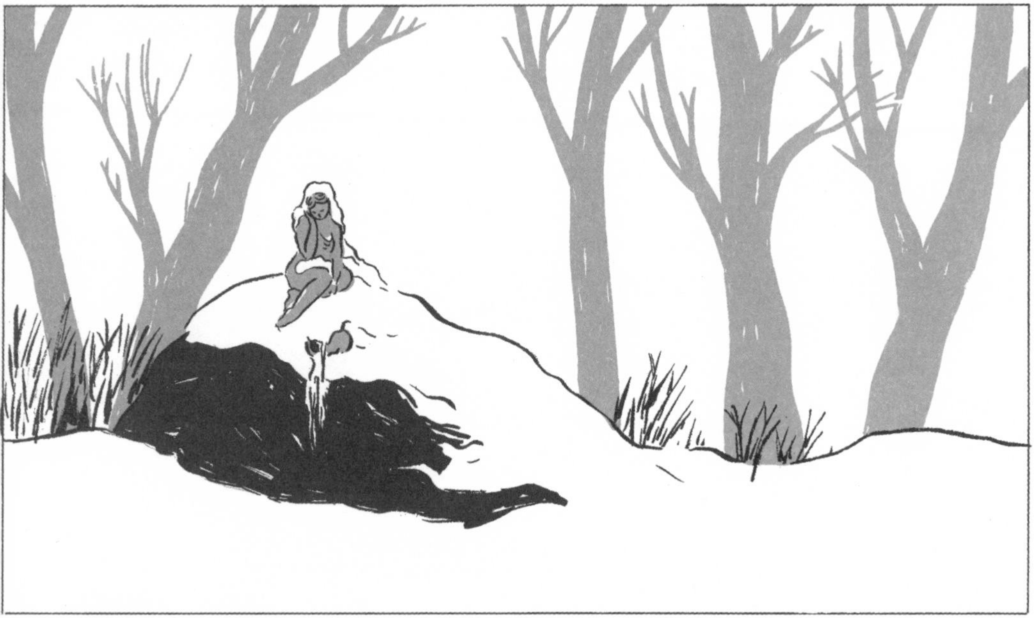

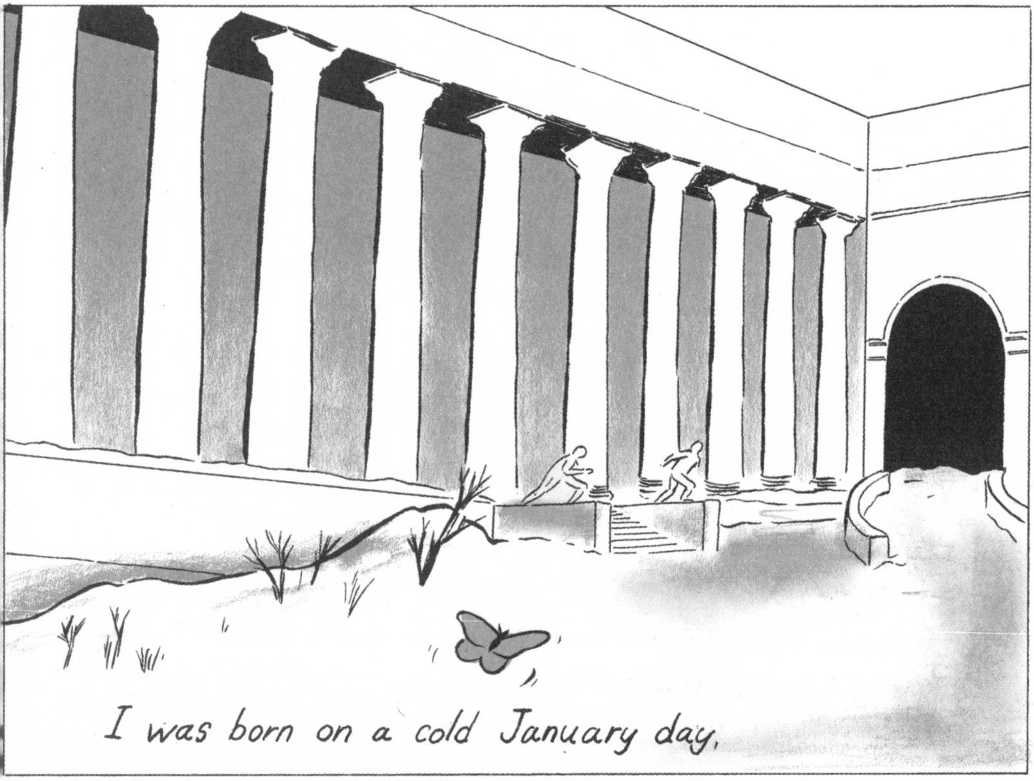
I was born on a cold January day.

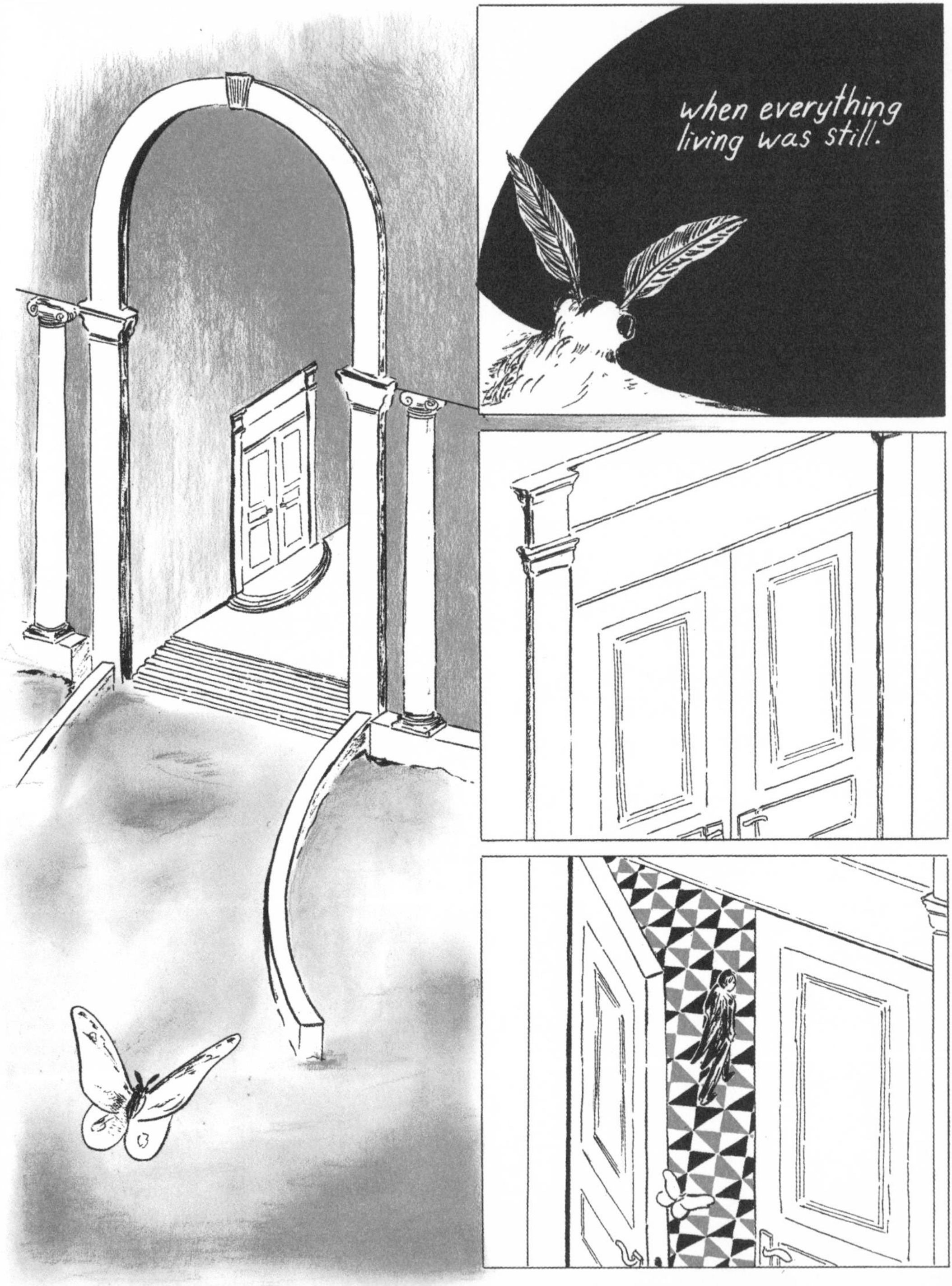
when everything living was still.

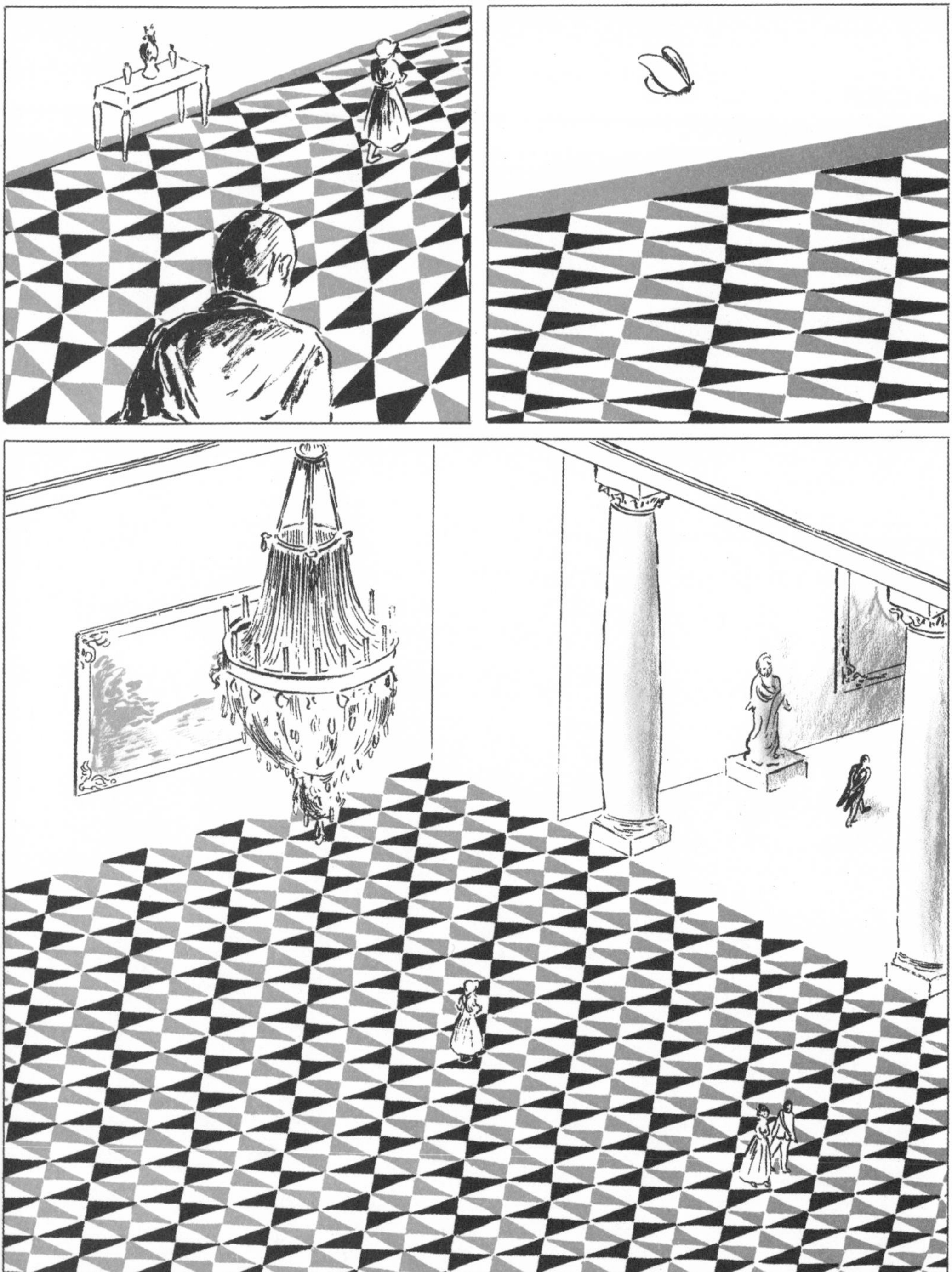

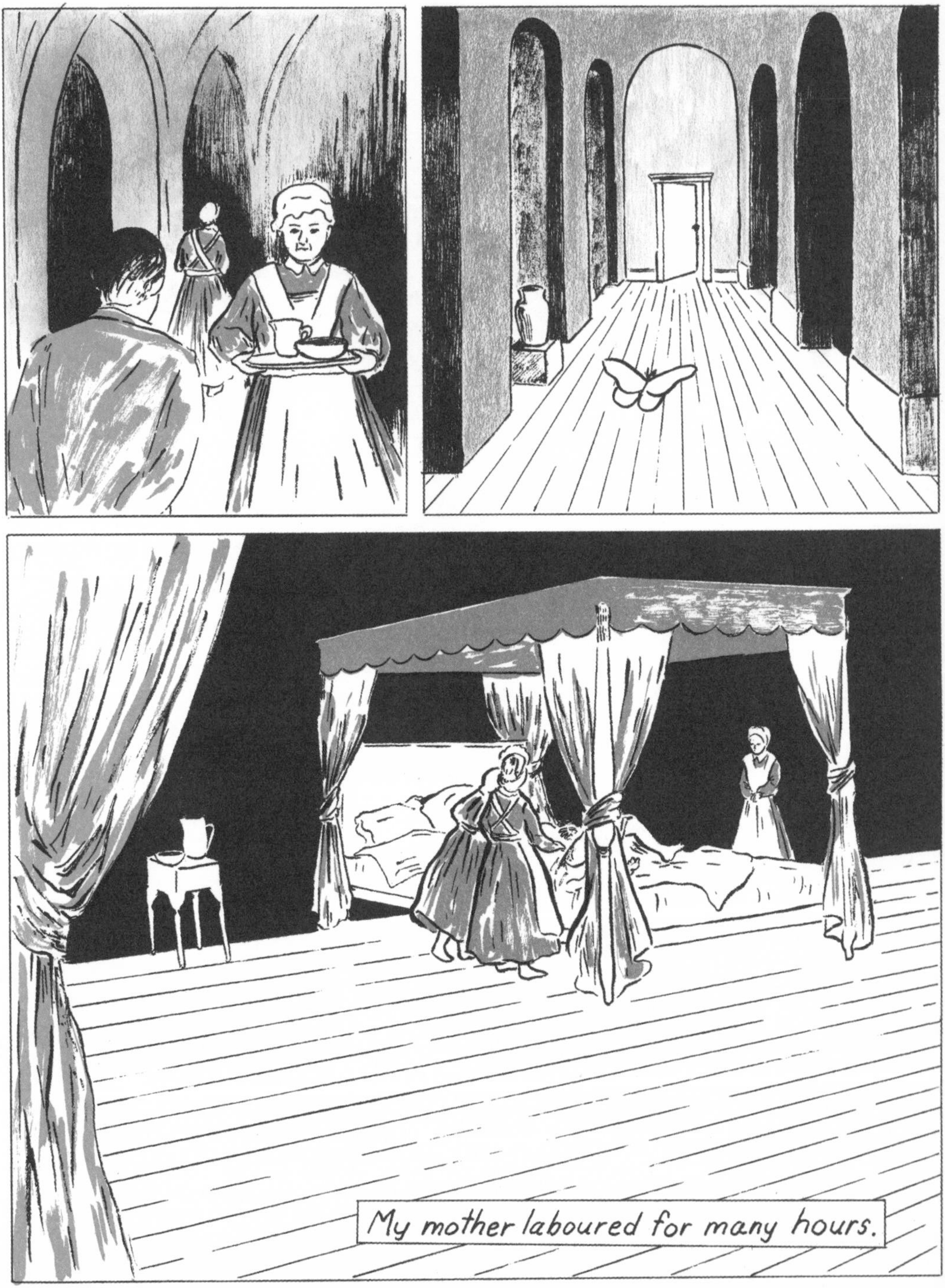
My mother laboured for many hours.

I was a fourth daughter,

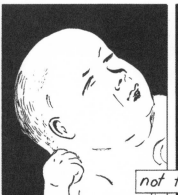

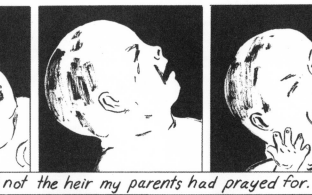

not the heir my parents had prayed for.

The midwife carried me away to the nursery.

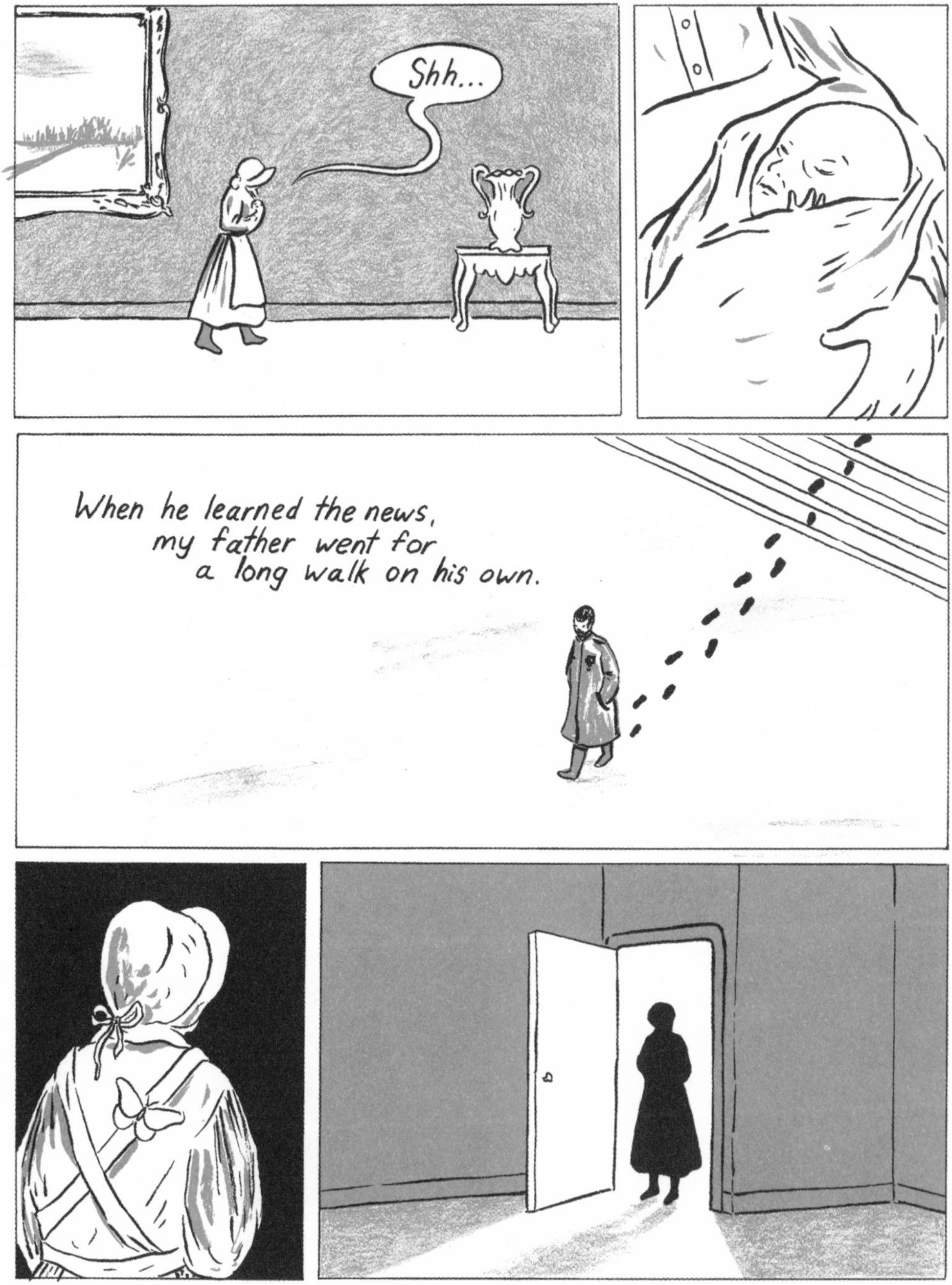
Shh...
When he learned the news, my father went for a long walk on his own.

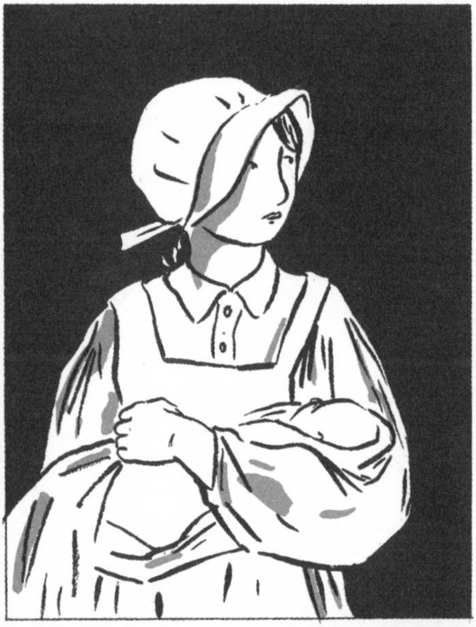
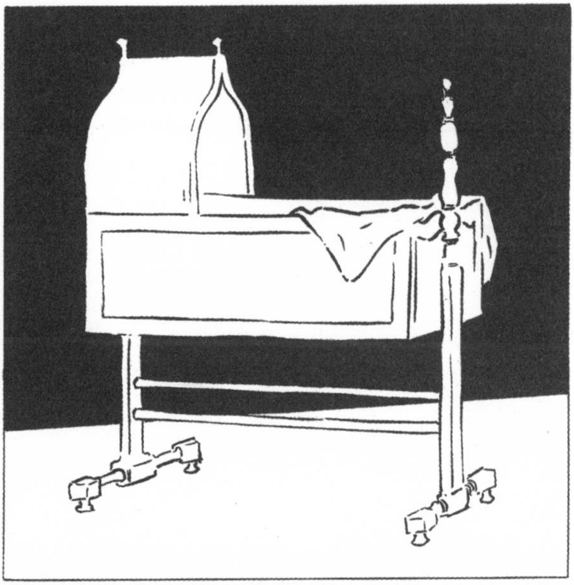
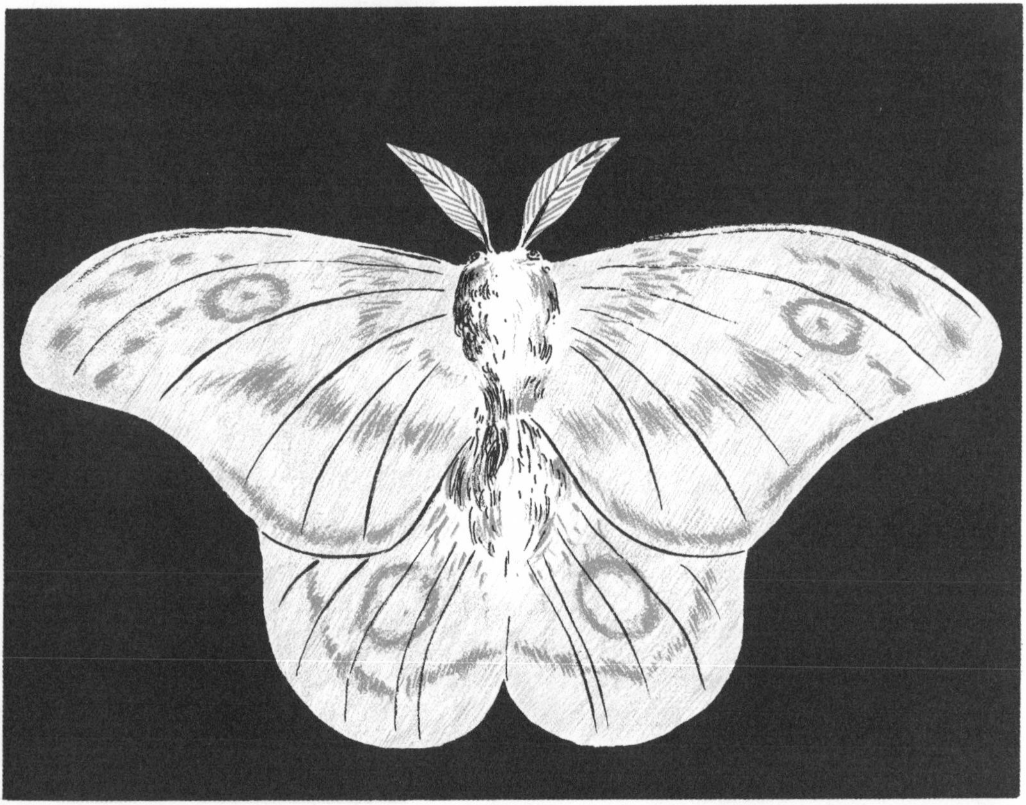

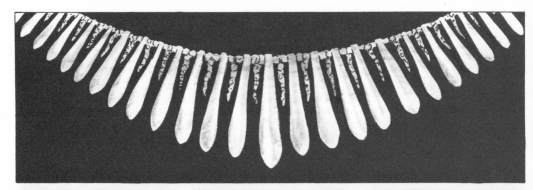

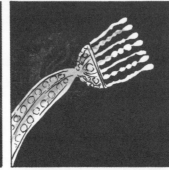

Still, no expense was spared at my christening, where I was declared Anastasia Nikolaevna, Grand Duchess of Russia.

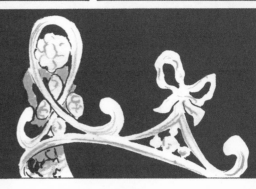

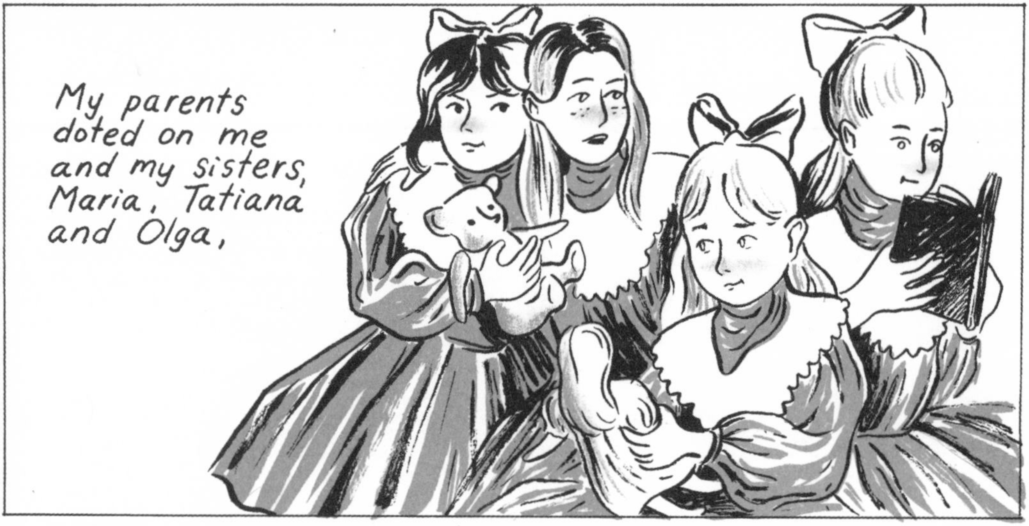
My parents doted on me and my sisters, Maria, Tatiana and Olga,

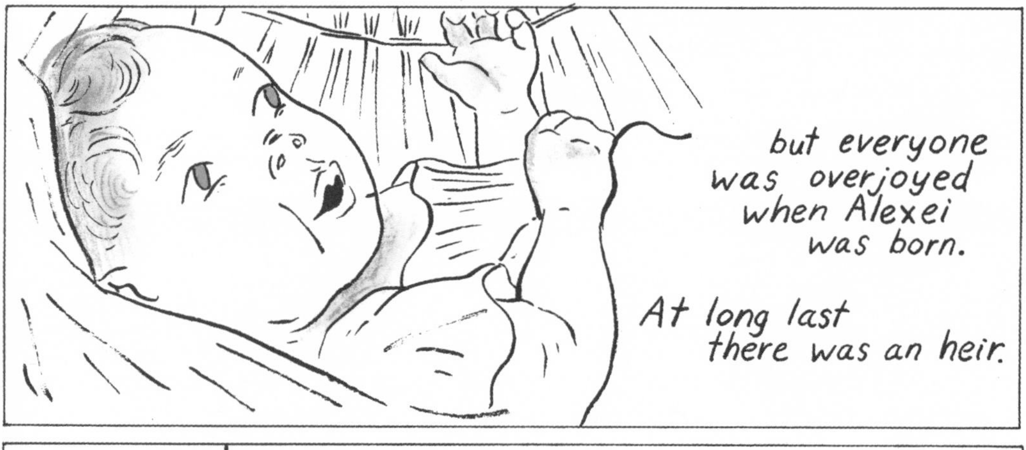
but everyone was overjoyed when Alexei was born.
At long last there was an heir.

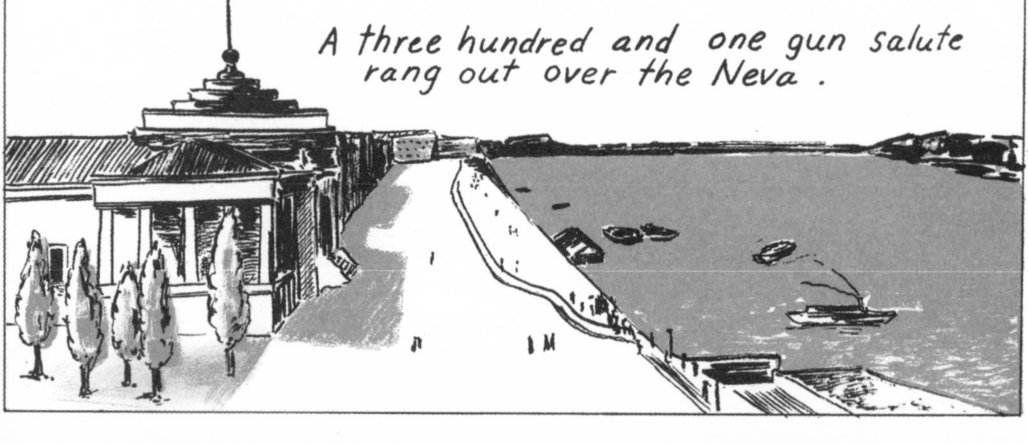
A three hundred and one gun salute rang out over the Neva .

It soon became clear, though, that my baby brother was not well.

Mama!

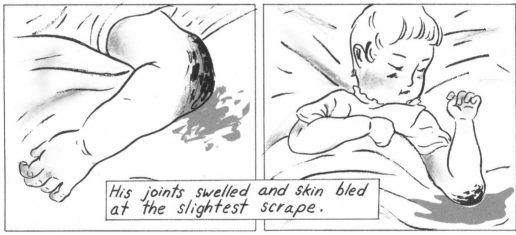

His joints swelled and skin bled at the slightest scrape.

My parents hid his condition from even our closest relatives.

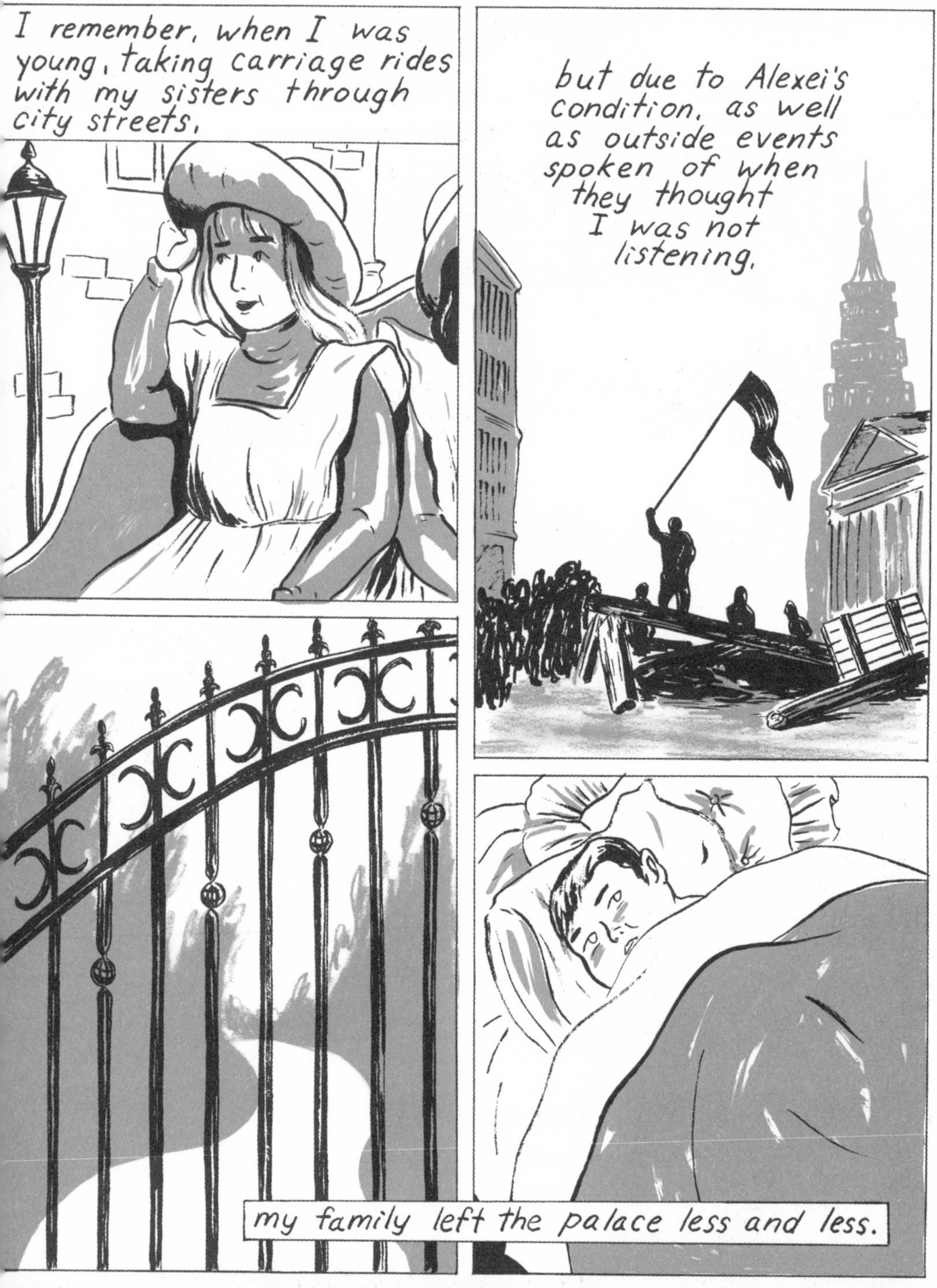
I remember, when I was young, taking carriage rides with my sisters through city streets,
but due to Alexei's condition, as well as outside events spoken of when they thought I was not listening,
my family left the palace less and less.

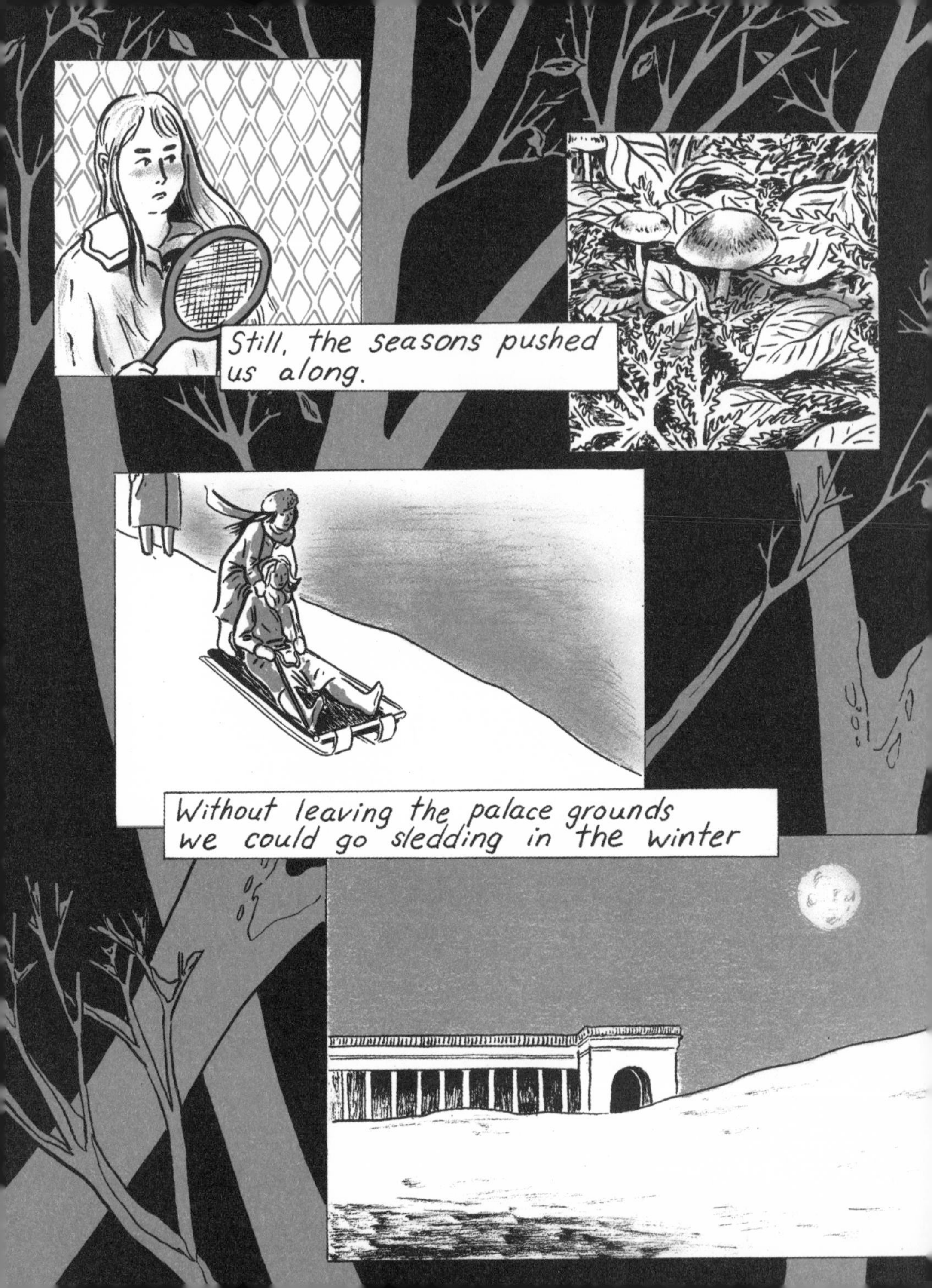
Still, the seasons pushed us along.
Without leaving the palace grounds we could go sledding in the winter

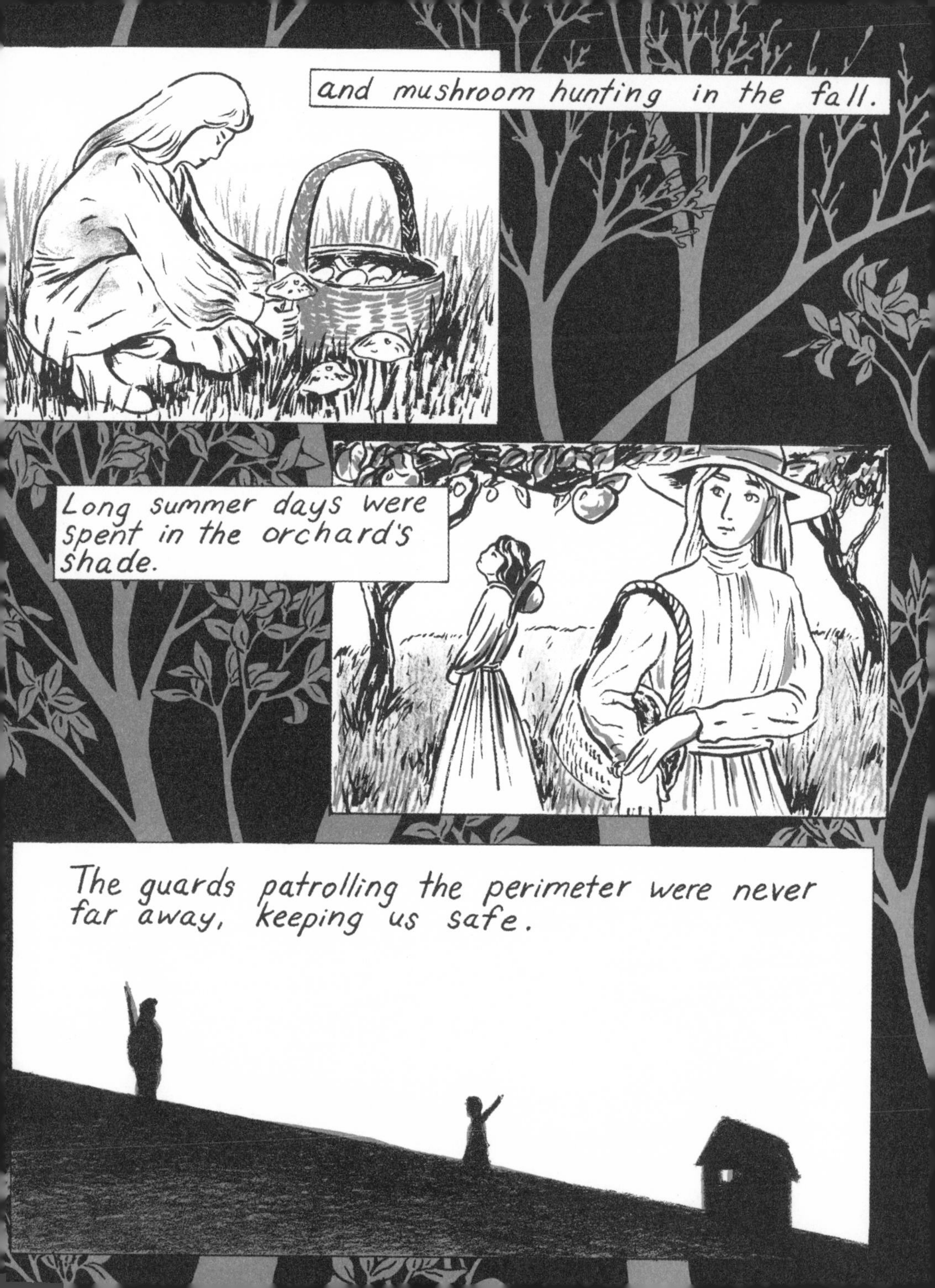
and mushroom hunting in the fall.
Long summer days were spent in the orchard's shade.
The guards patrolling the perimeter were never far away, keeping us safe.

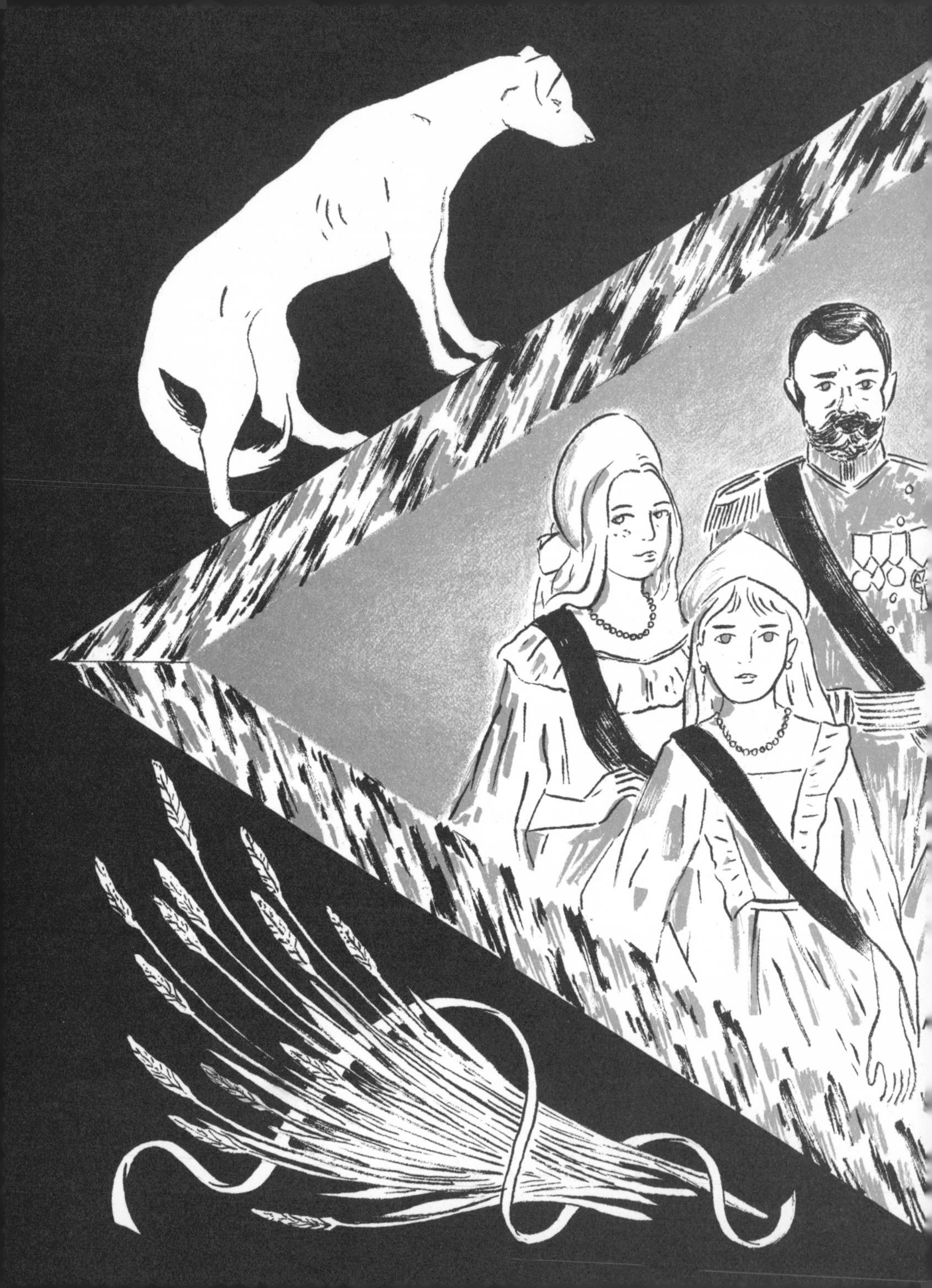

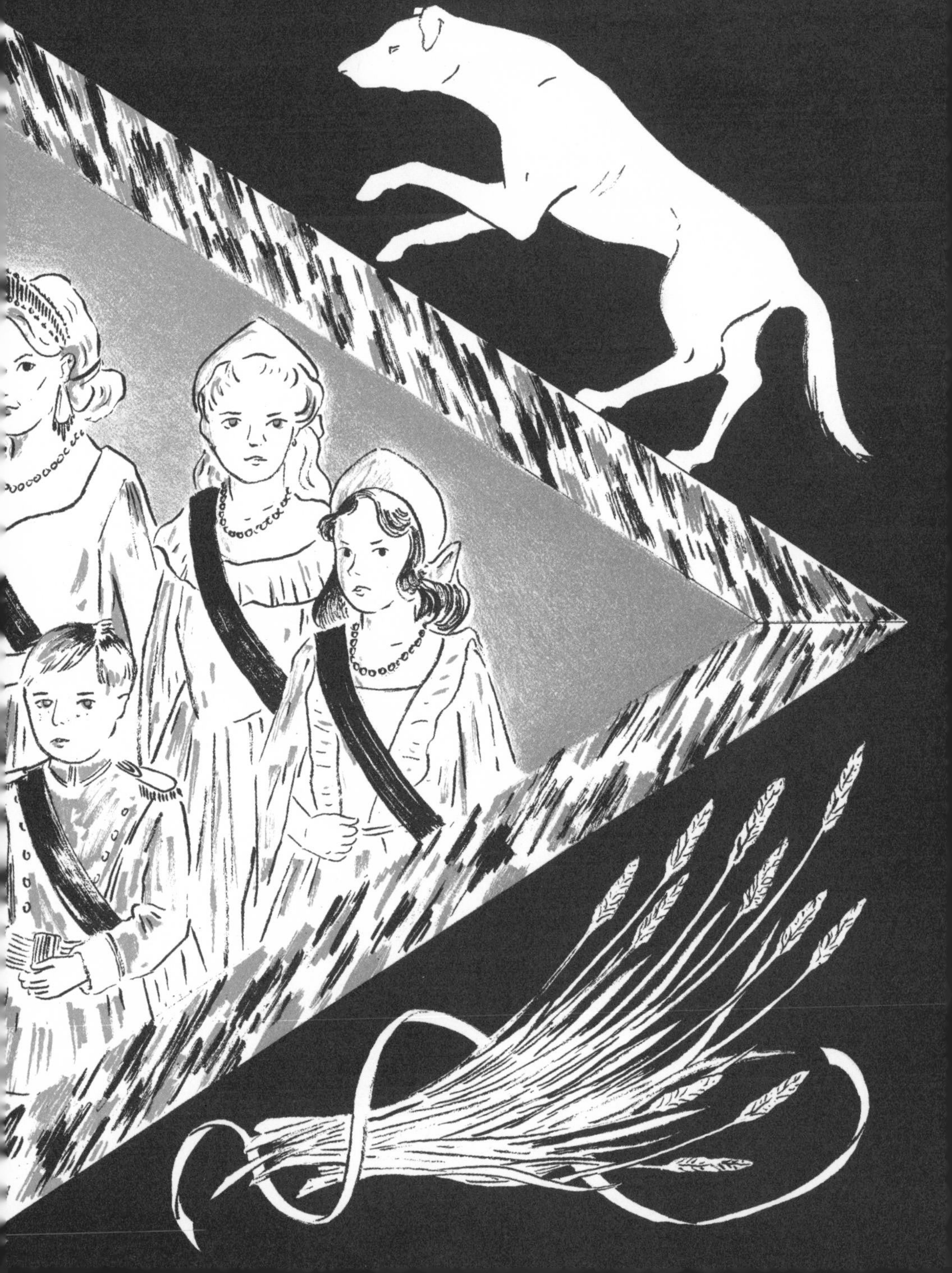

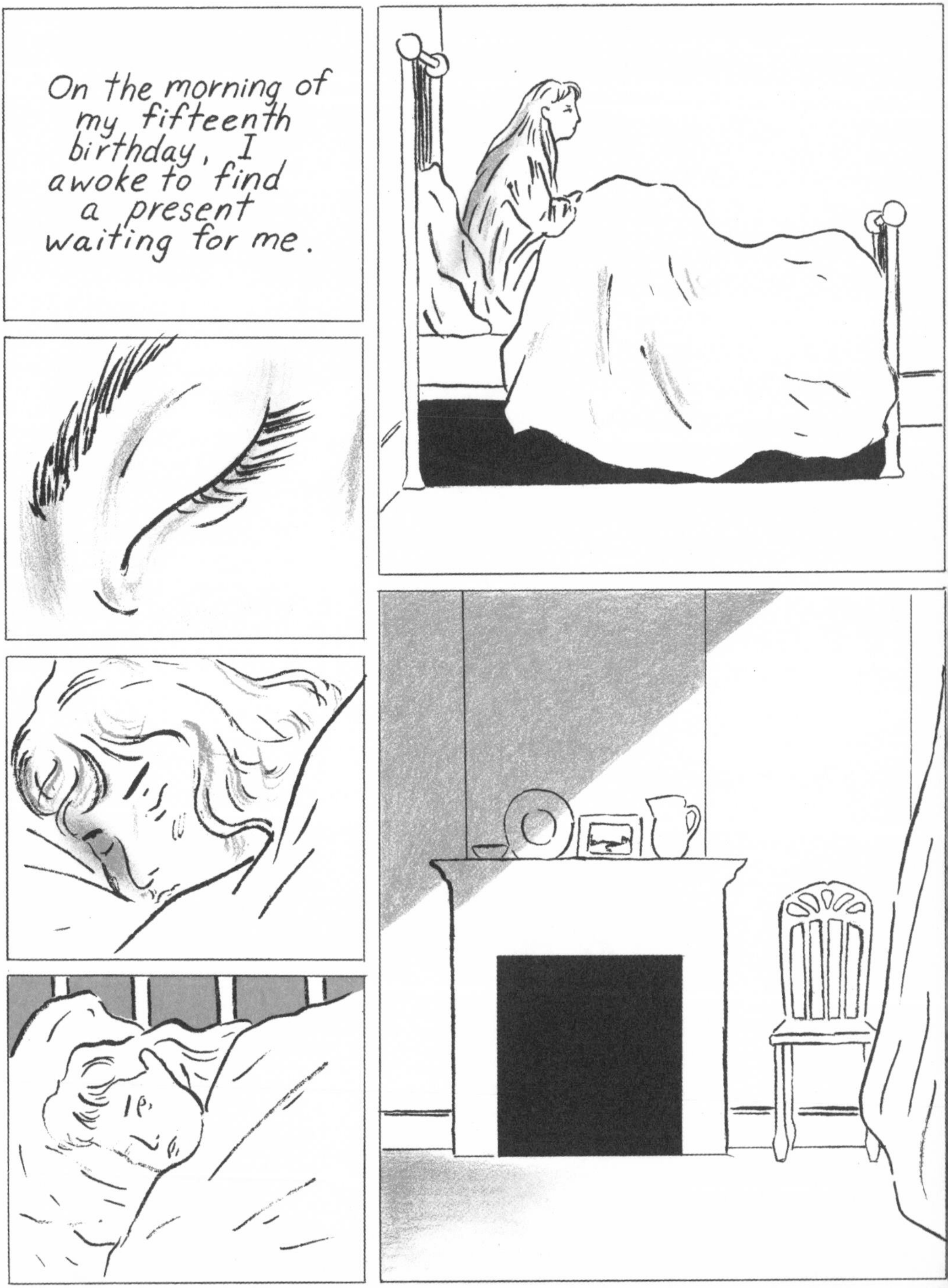
On the morning of my fifteenth birthday, I awoke to find a present waiting for me.

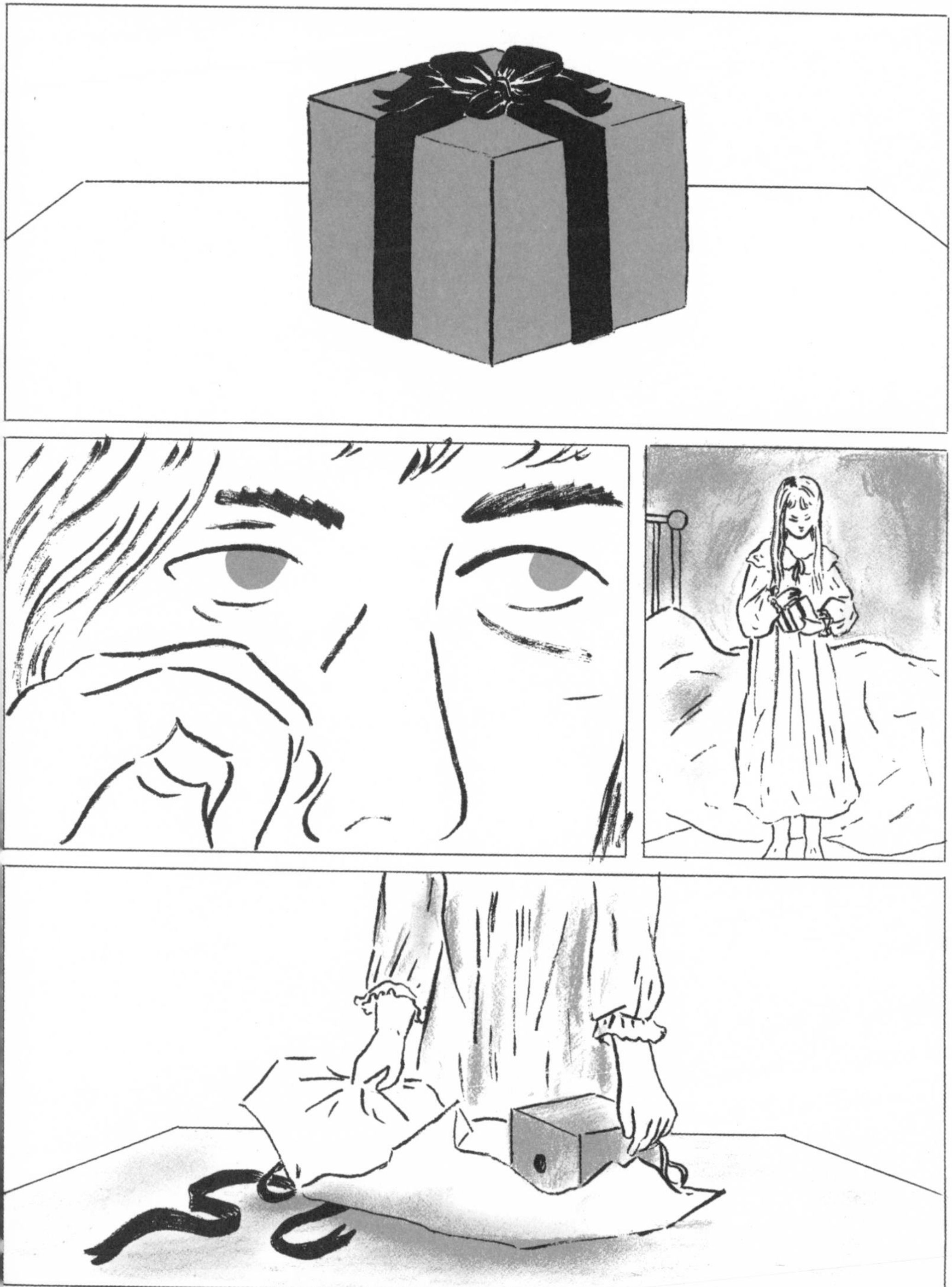

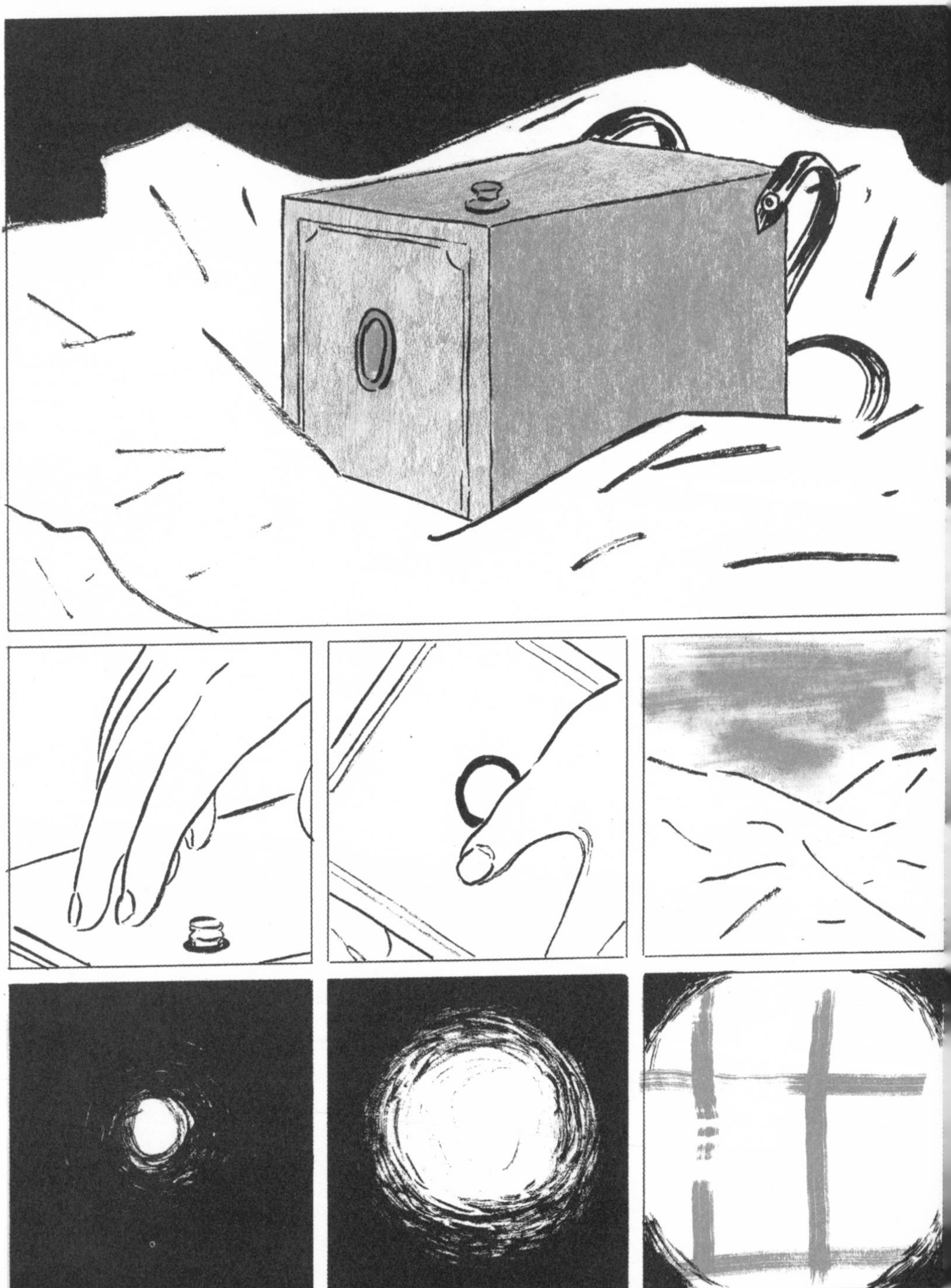

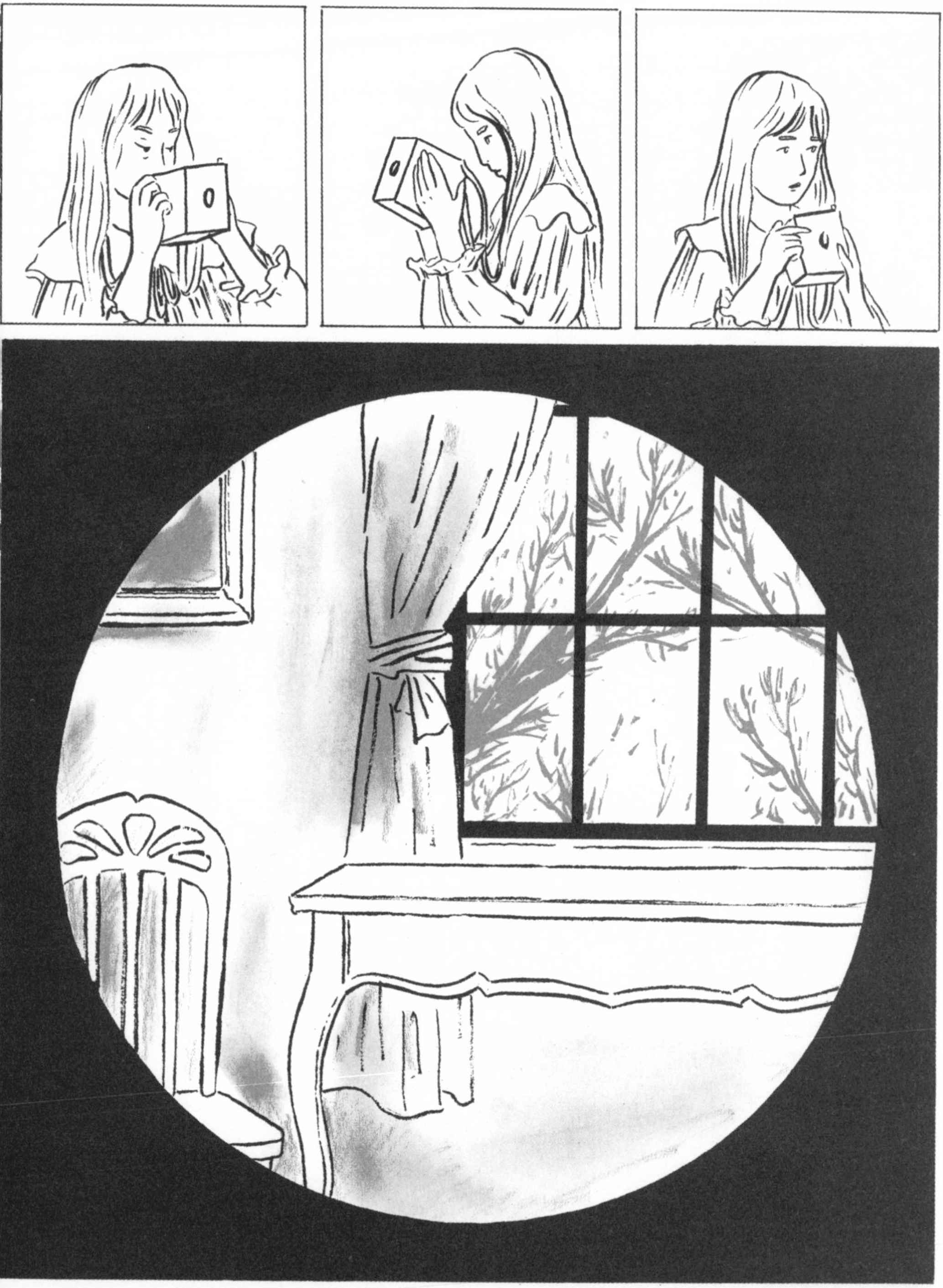

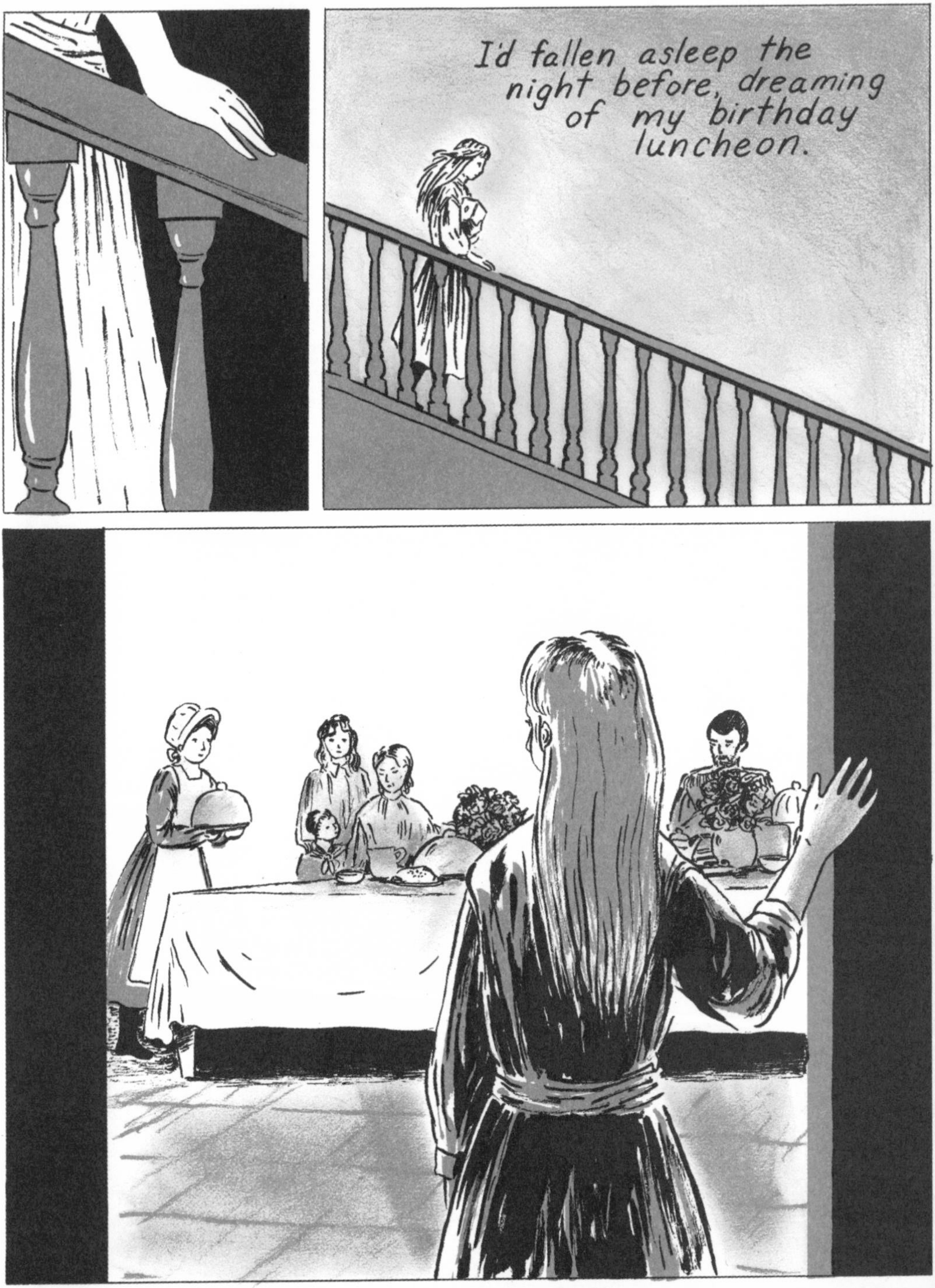
I'd fallen asleep the night before, dreaming of my birthday luncheon.

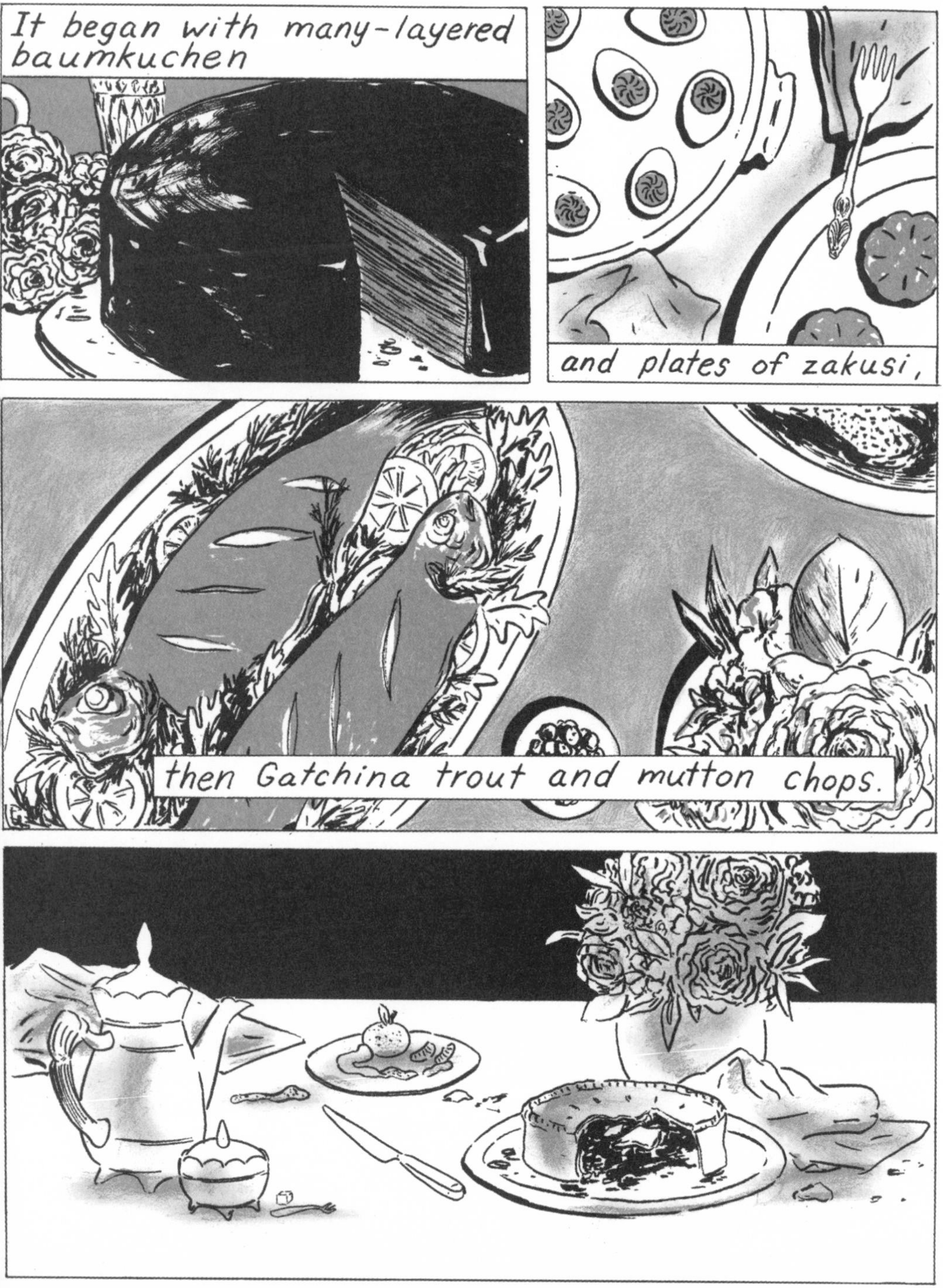
It began with many-layered baumkuchen
and plates of zakusi,
then Gatchina trout and mutton chops.

By the time the coffee course had finished I couldn't eat another bite.

To my surprise, no one could say who had sent the camera.

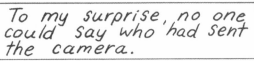

You press the shutter here I believe.

Outside, the previous night's snow blanketed the grounds.

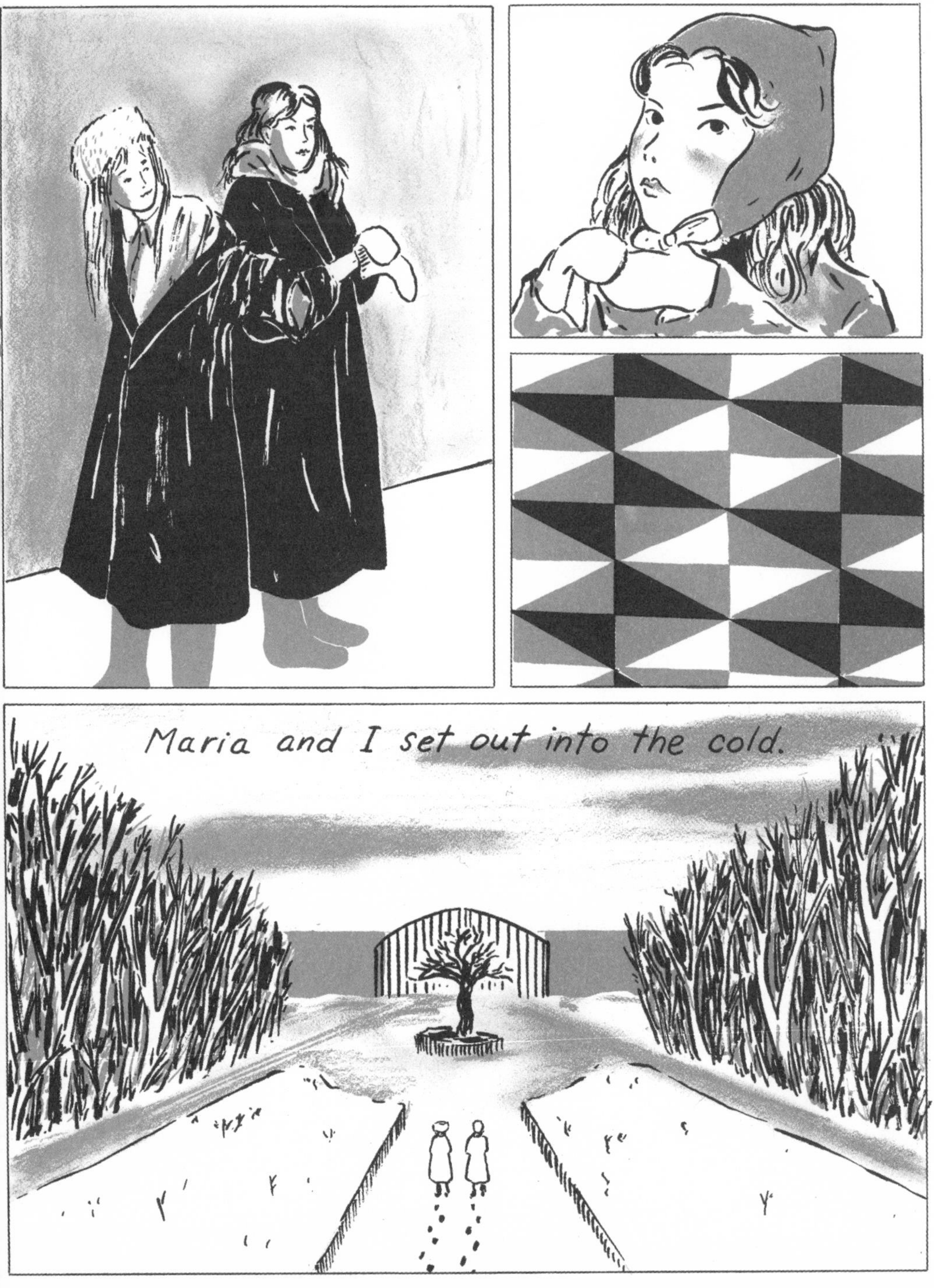
Maria and I set out into the cold.

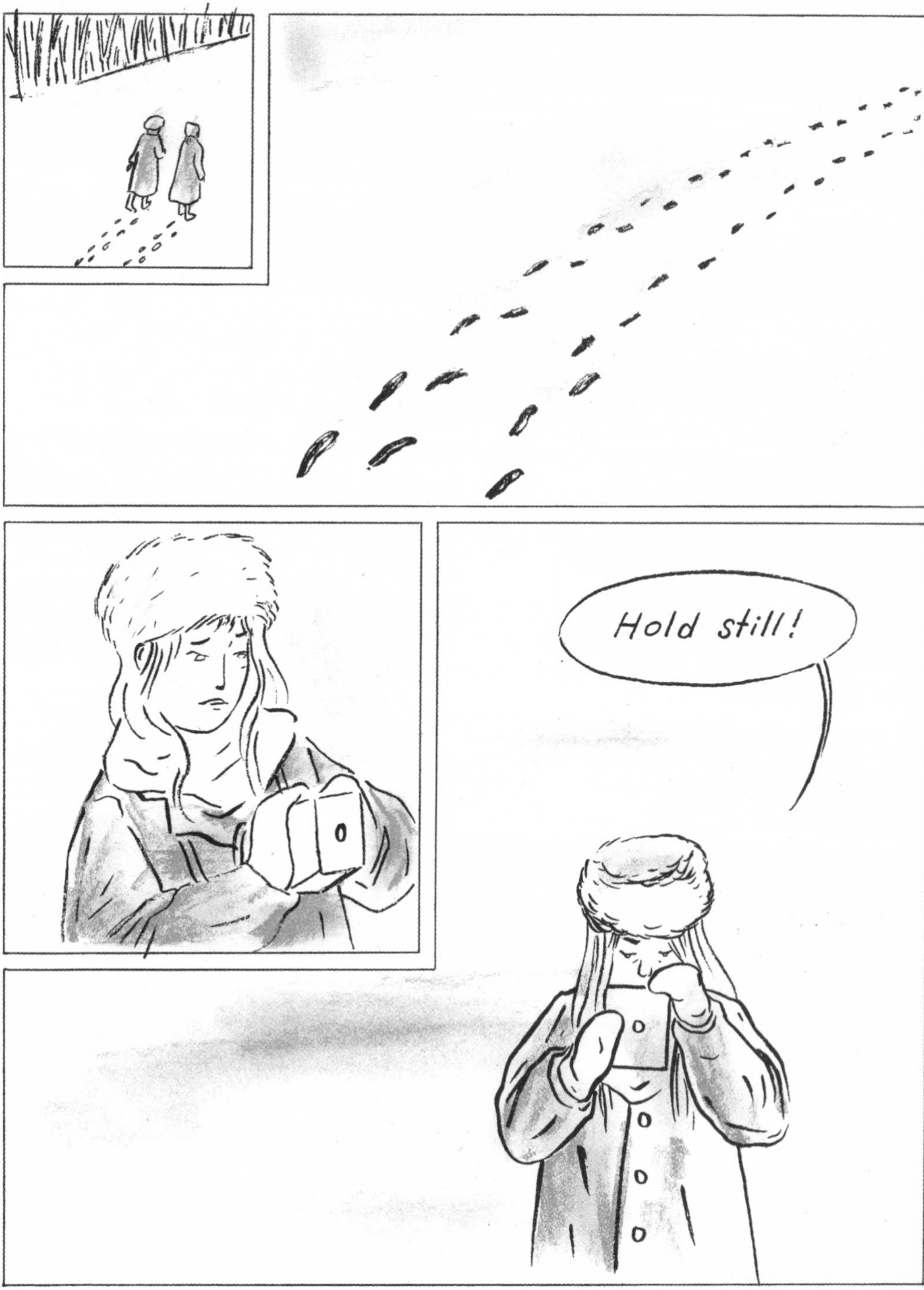
Hold still!

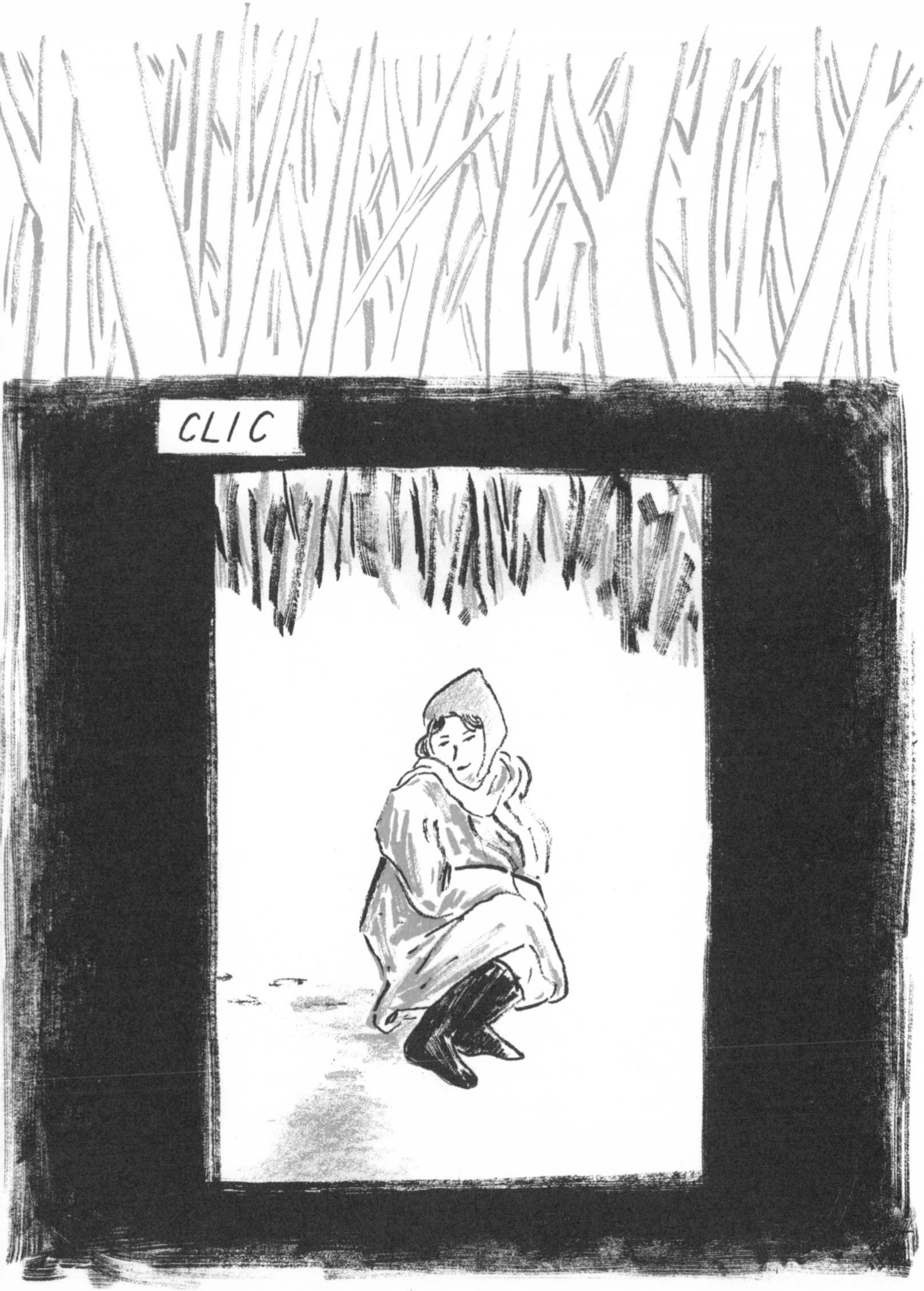
CLIC

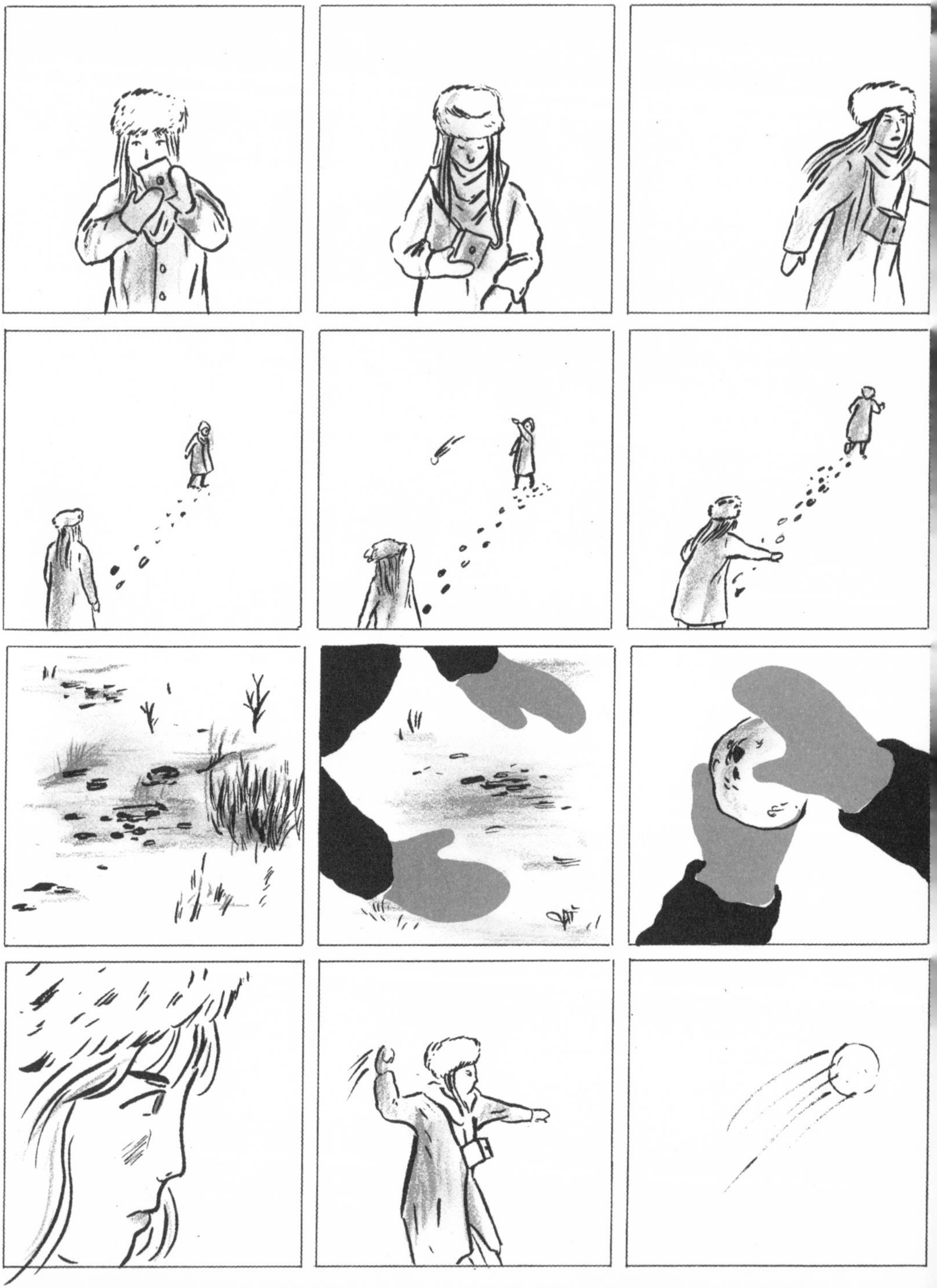

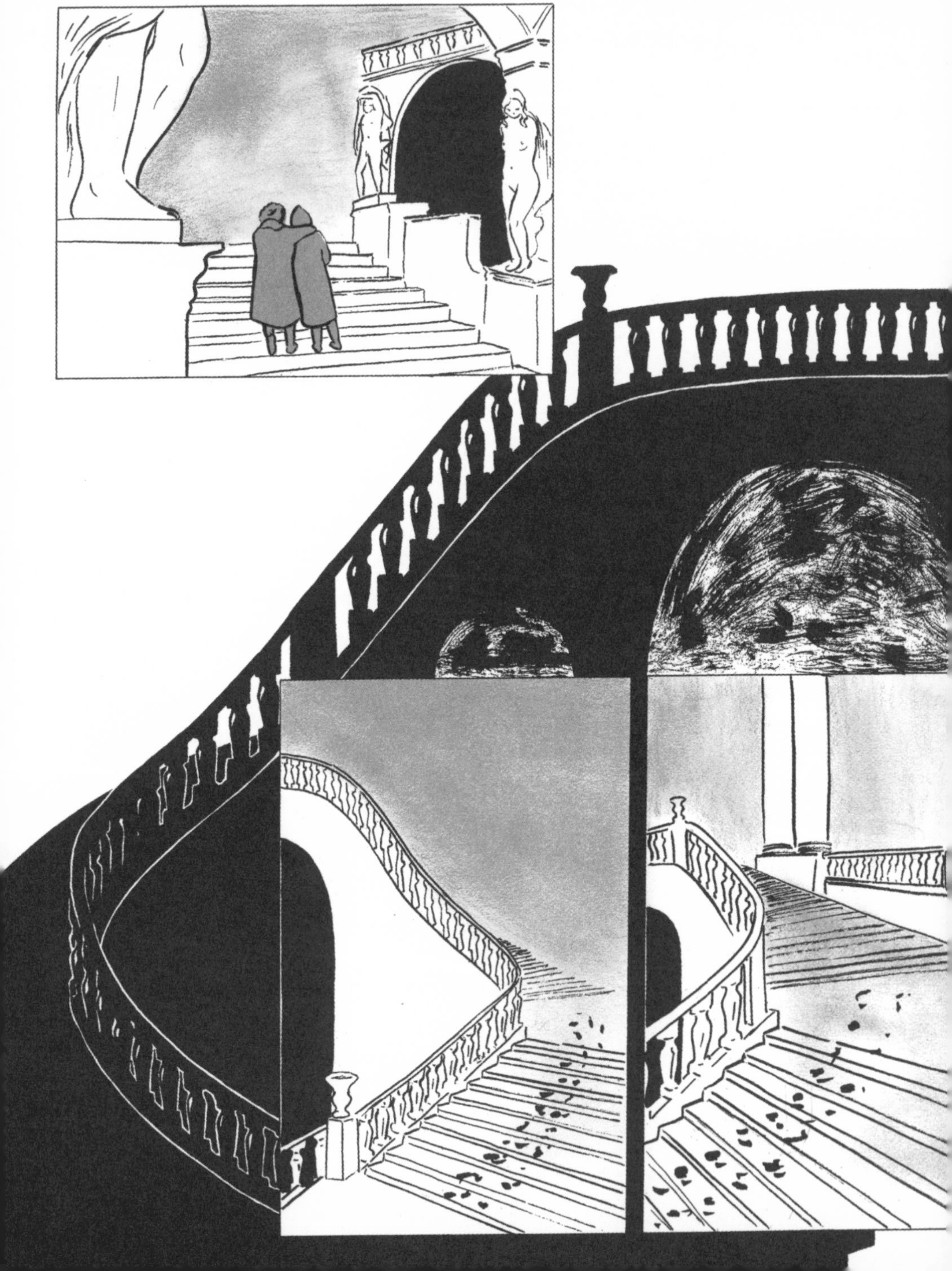

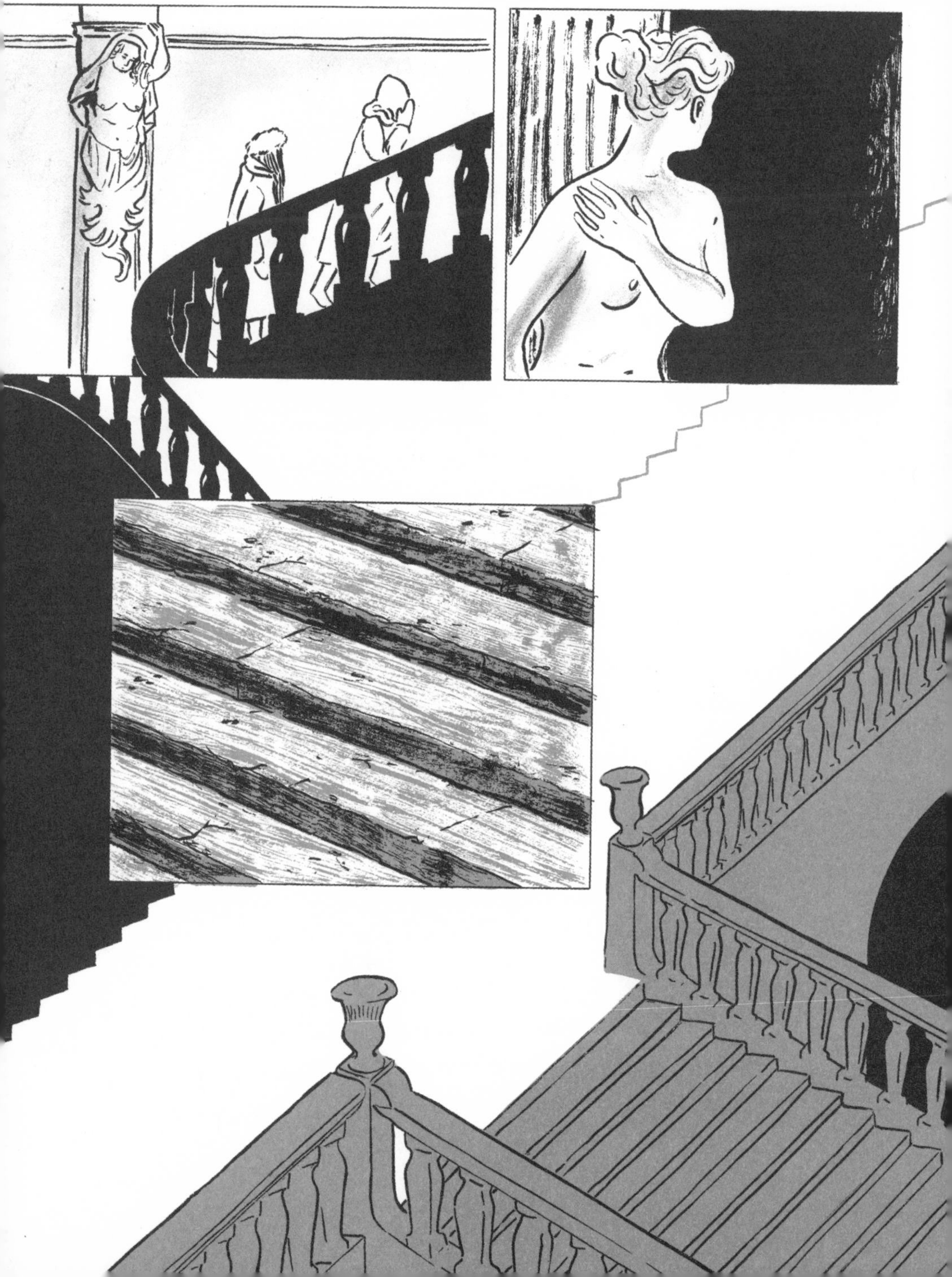

They all bleed
more than is
normal.

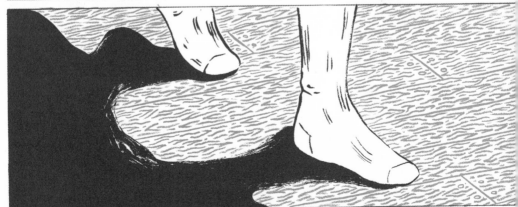

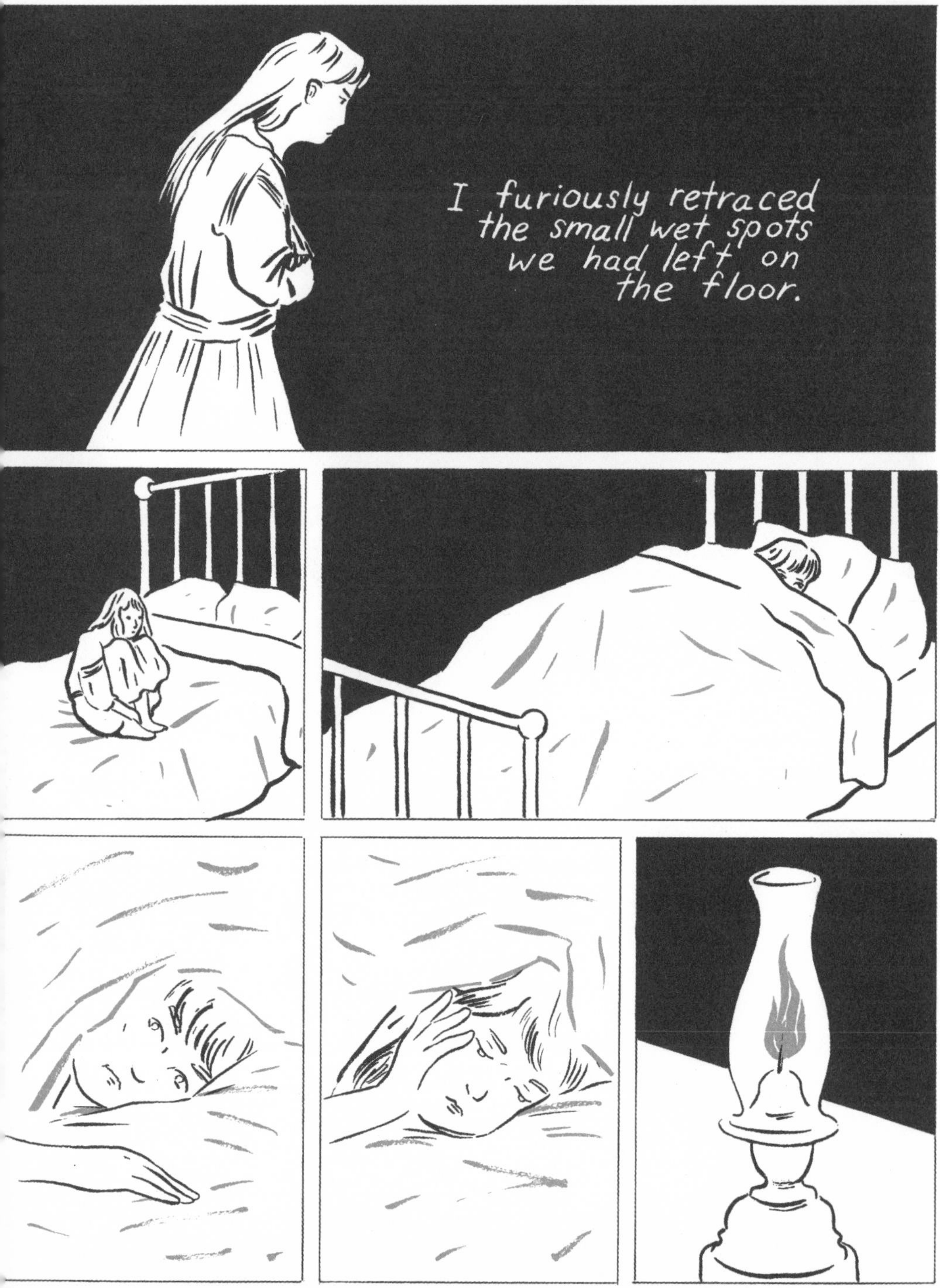
I furiously retraced the small wet spots we had left on the floor.

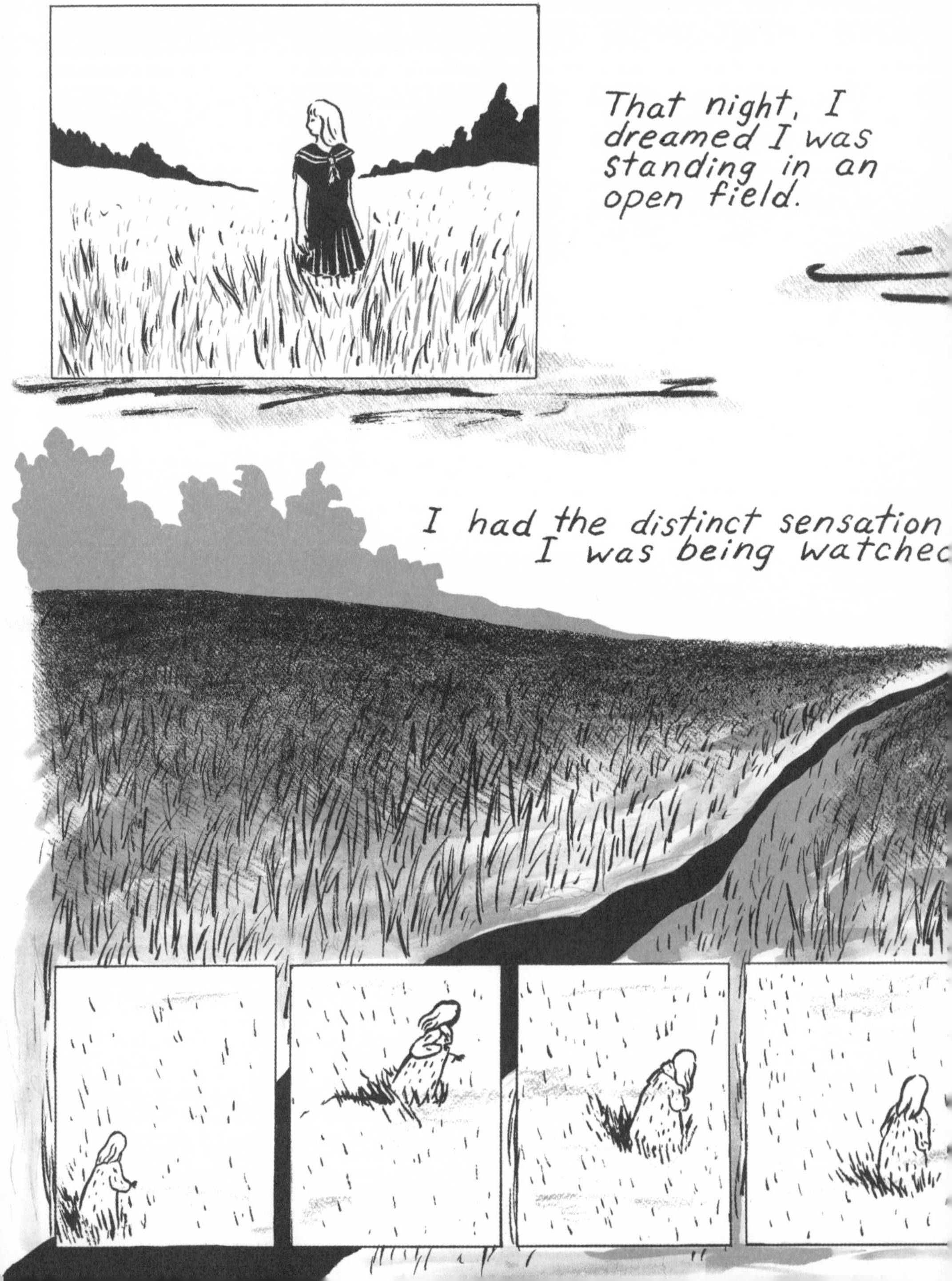
That night, I dreamed I was standing in an open field.
I had the distinct sensation I was being watche

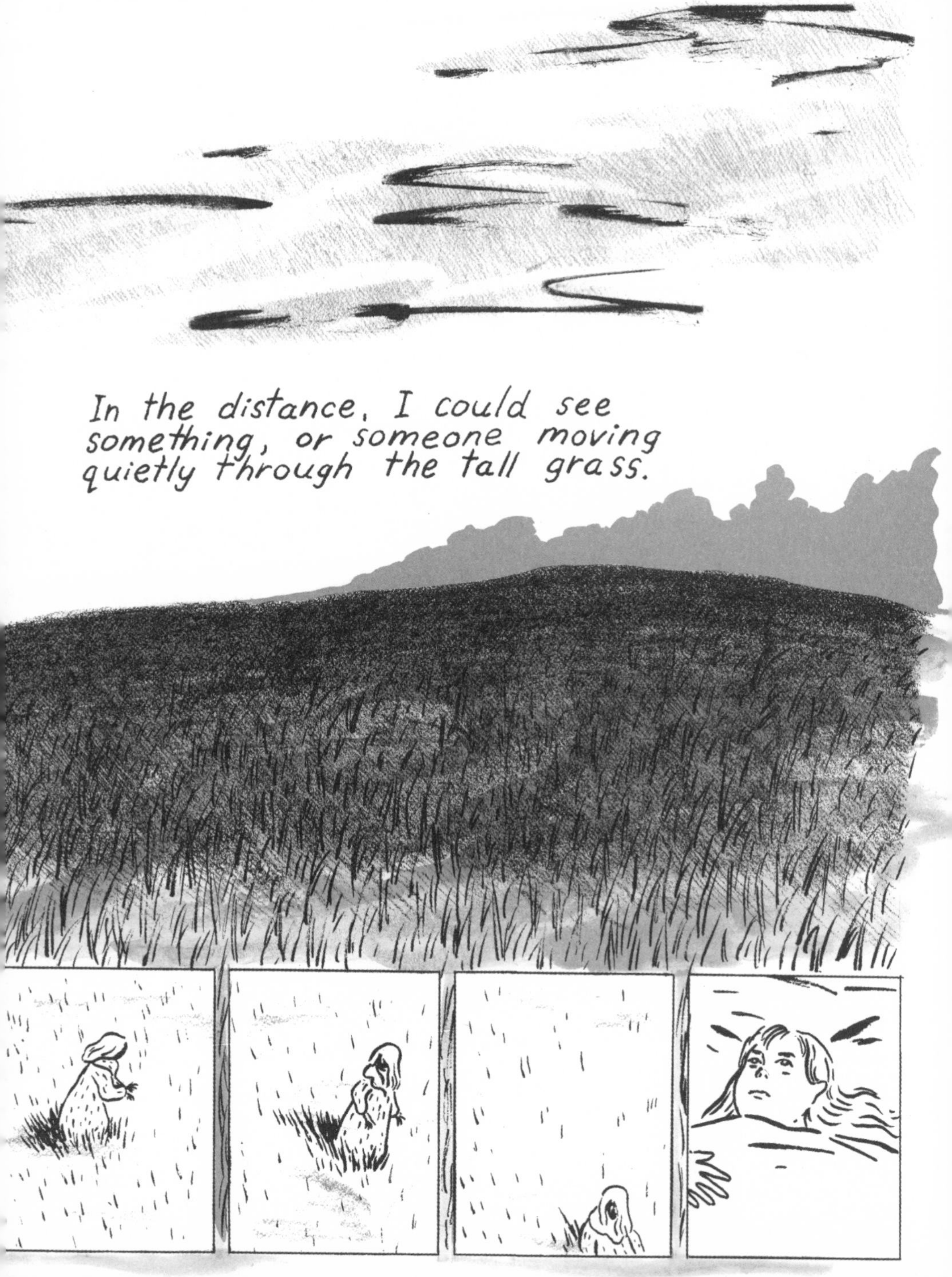
In the distance, I could see something, or someone moving quietly through the tall grass.

The next morning,

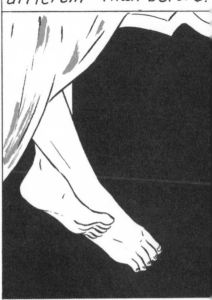

the world felt somehow different than before.

SKR SKR

Who had sent the camera? The guards kept a close eye on everything that came in and out.

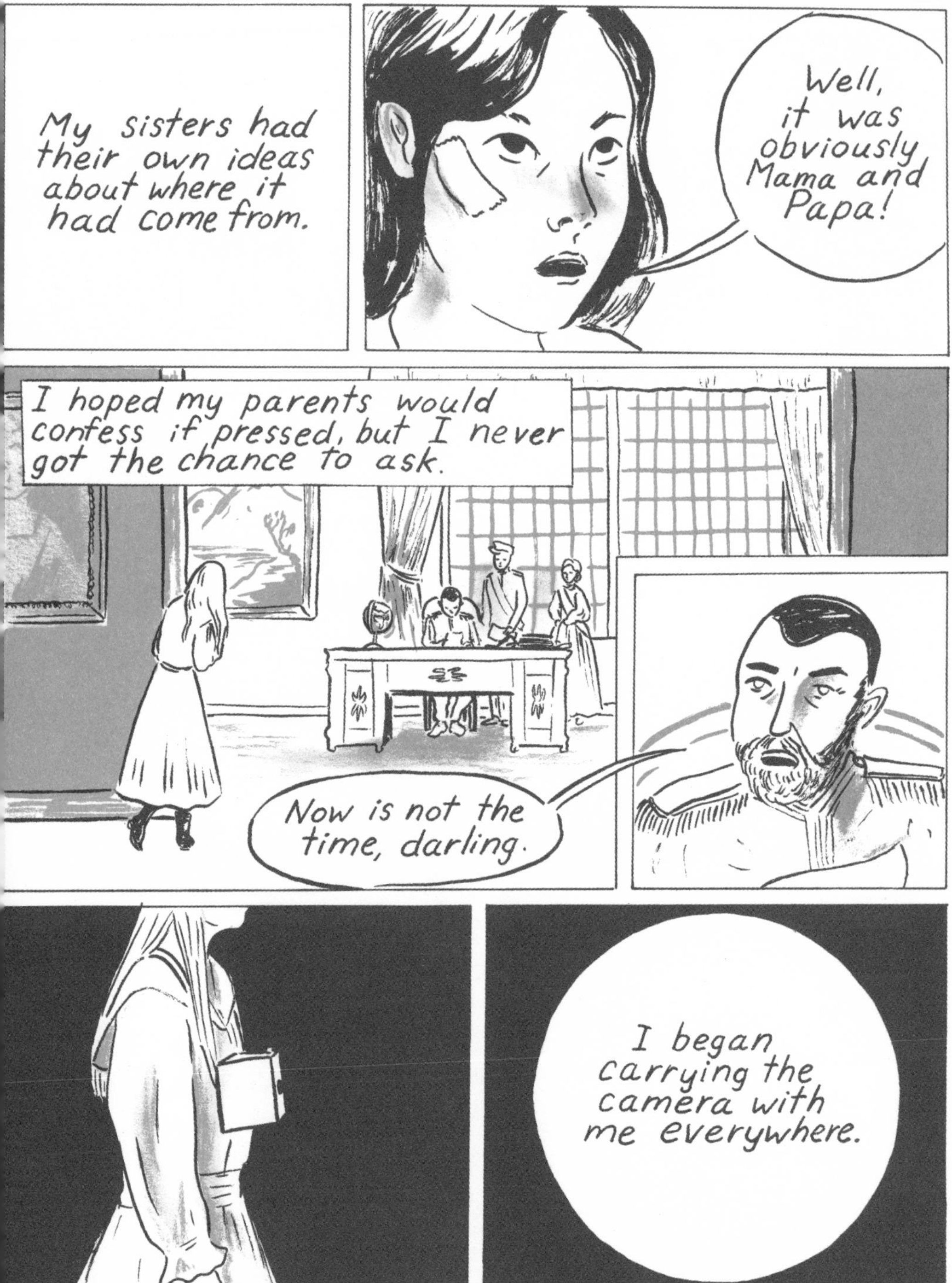
My sisters had their own ideas about where it had come from.
Well, it was obviously Mama and Papa!
I hoped my parents would confess if pressed, but I never got the chance to ask.
Now is not the time, darling.
I began carrying the camera with me everywhere.

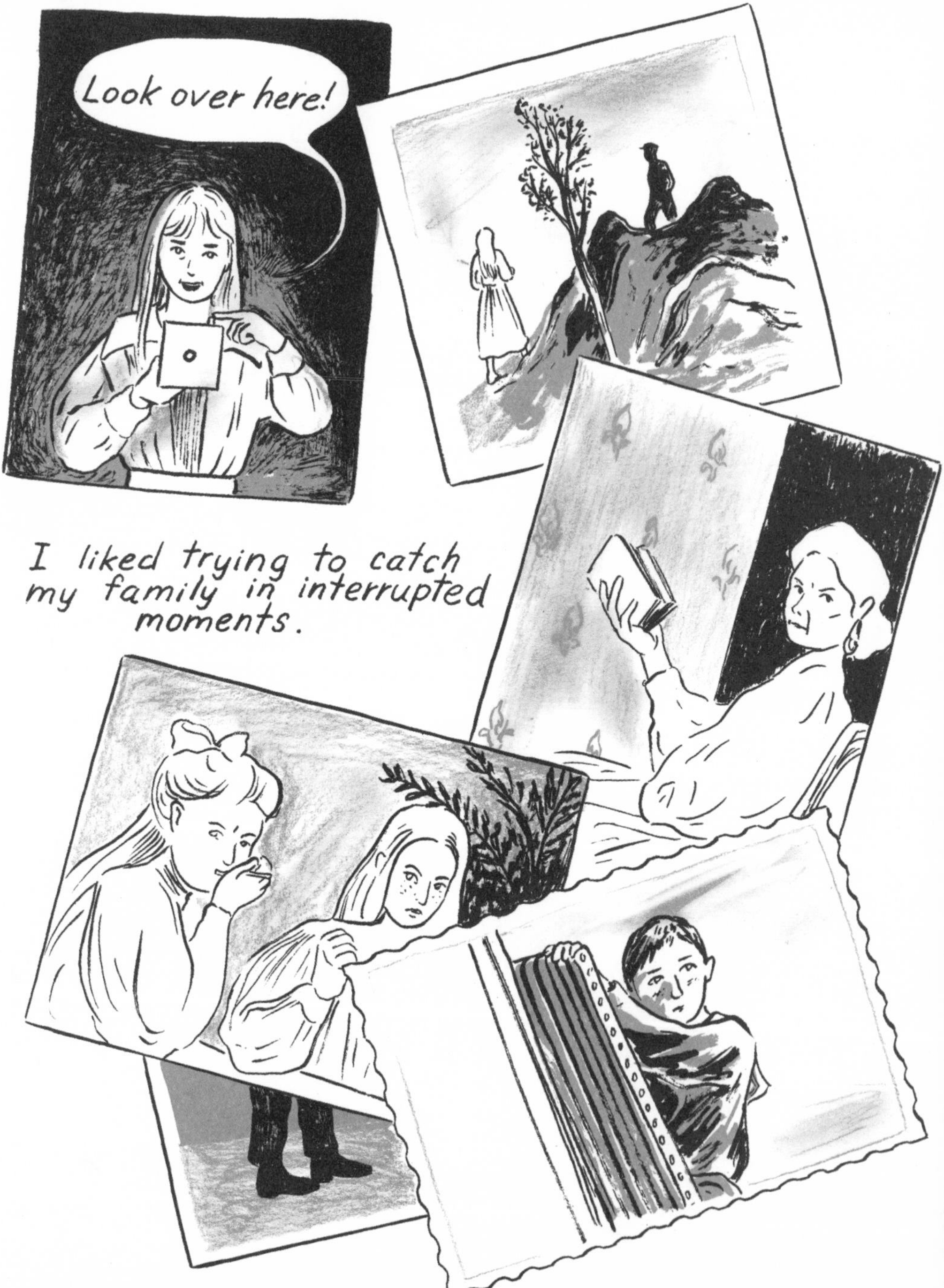
Look over here!
I liked trying to catch my family in interrupted moments.

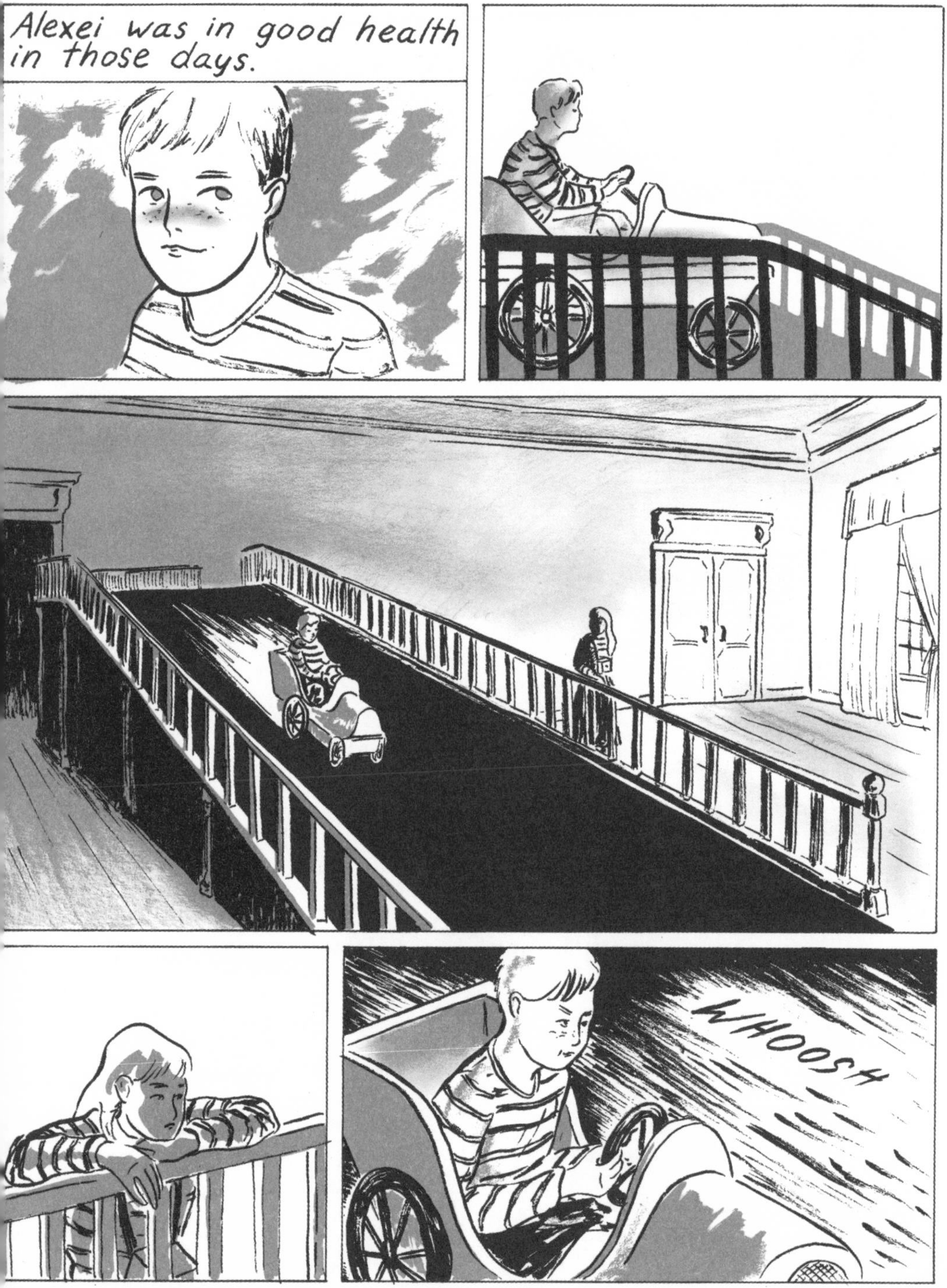

Alexei was in good health in those days.
WHOOSH

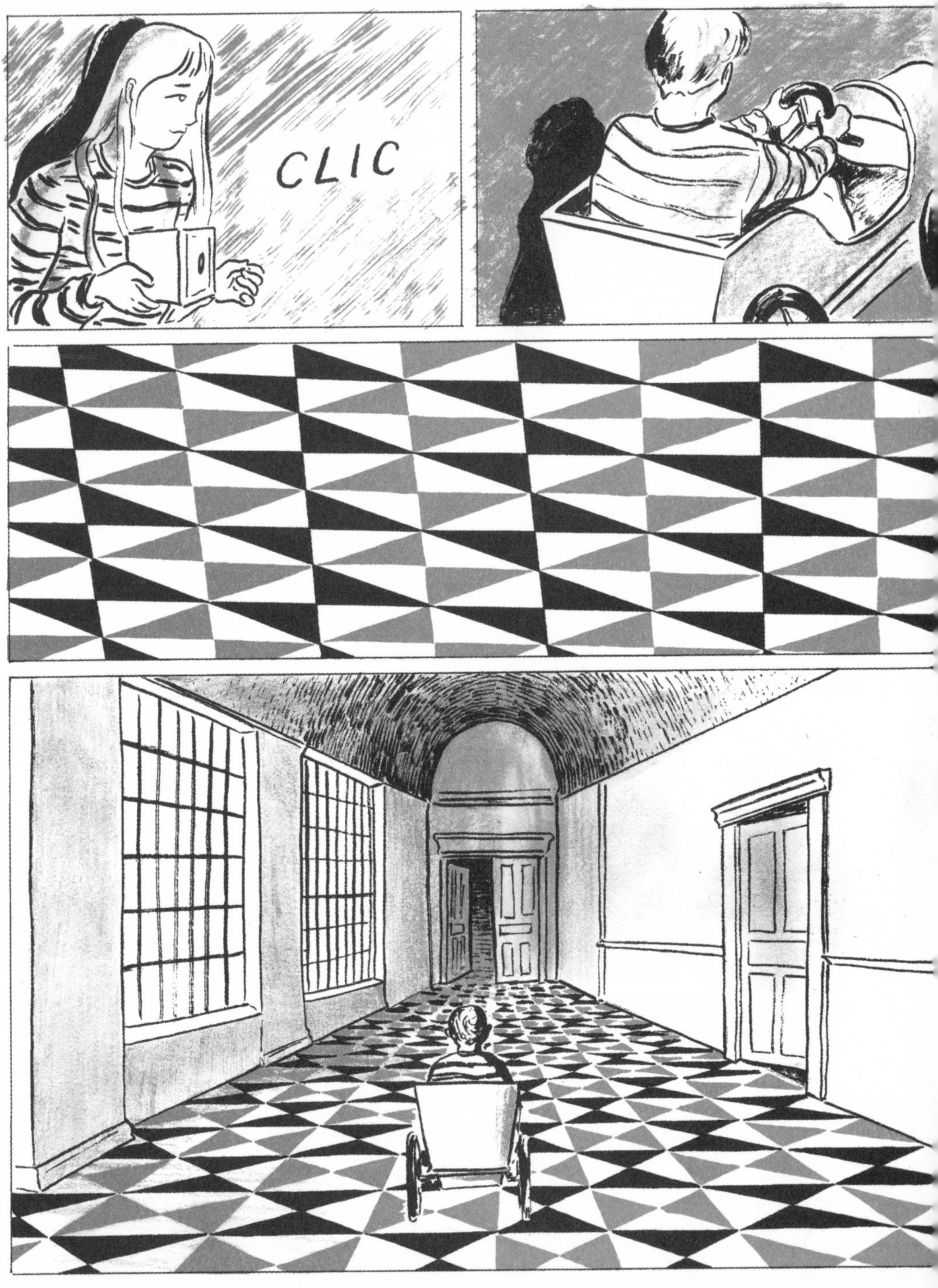
CLIC

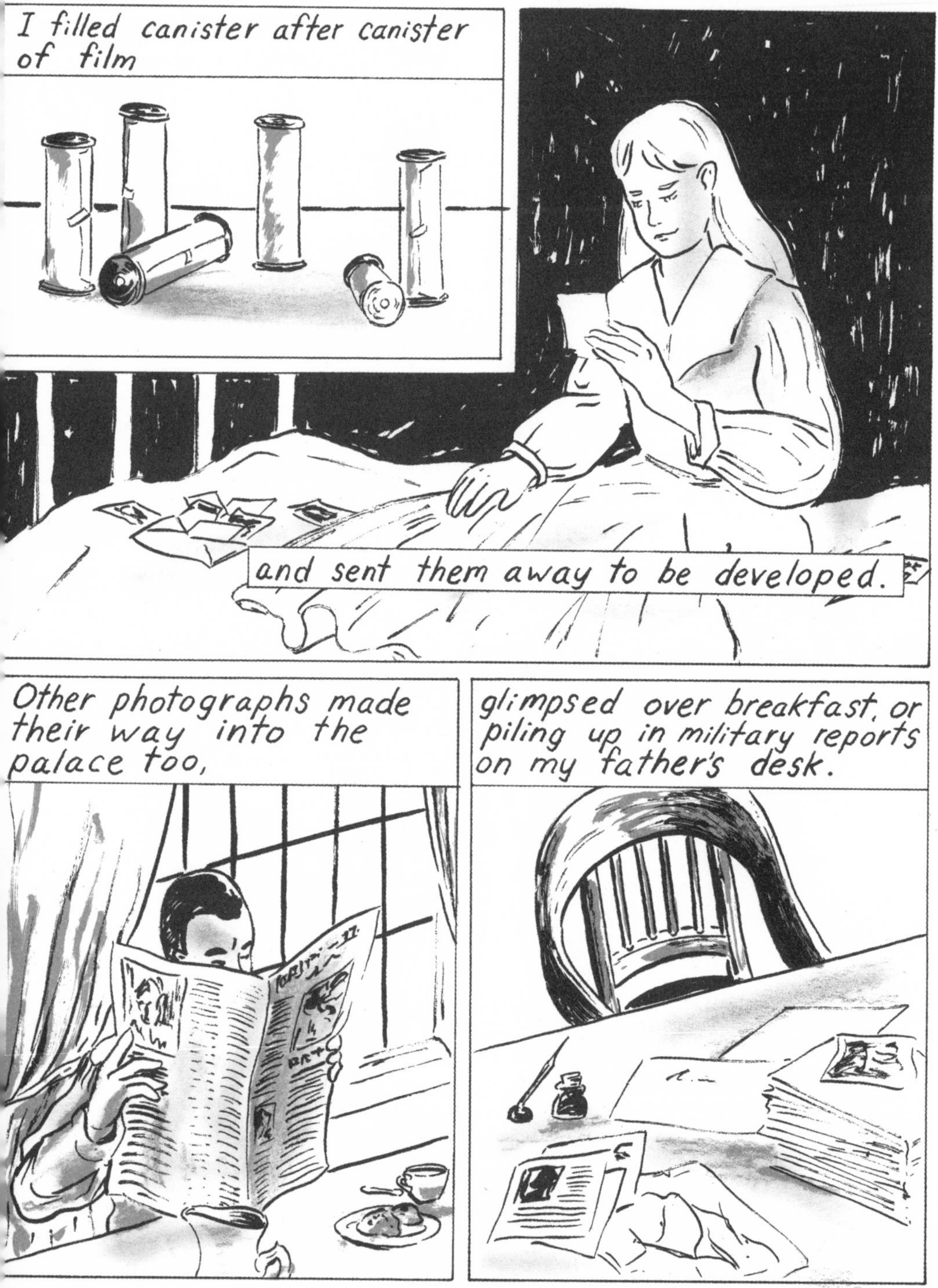
I filled canister after canister of film
and sent them away to be developed.
Other photographs made their way into the palace too,
glimpsed over breakfast, or piling up in military reports on my father's desk.

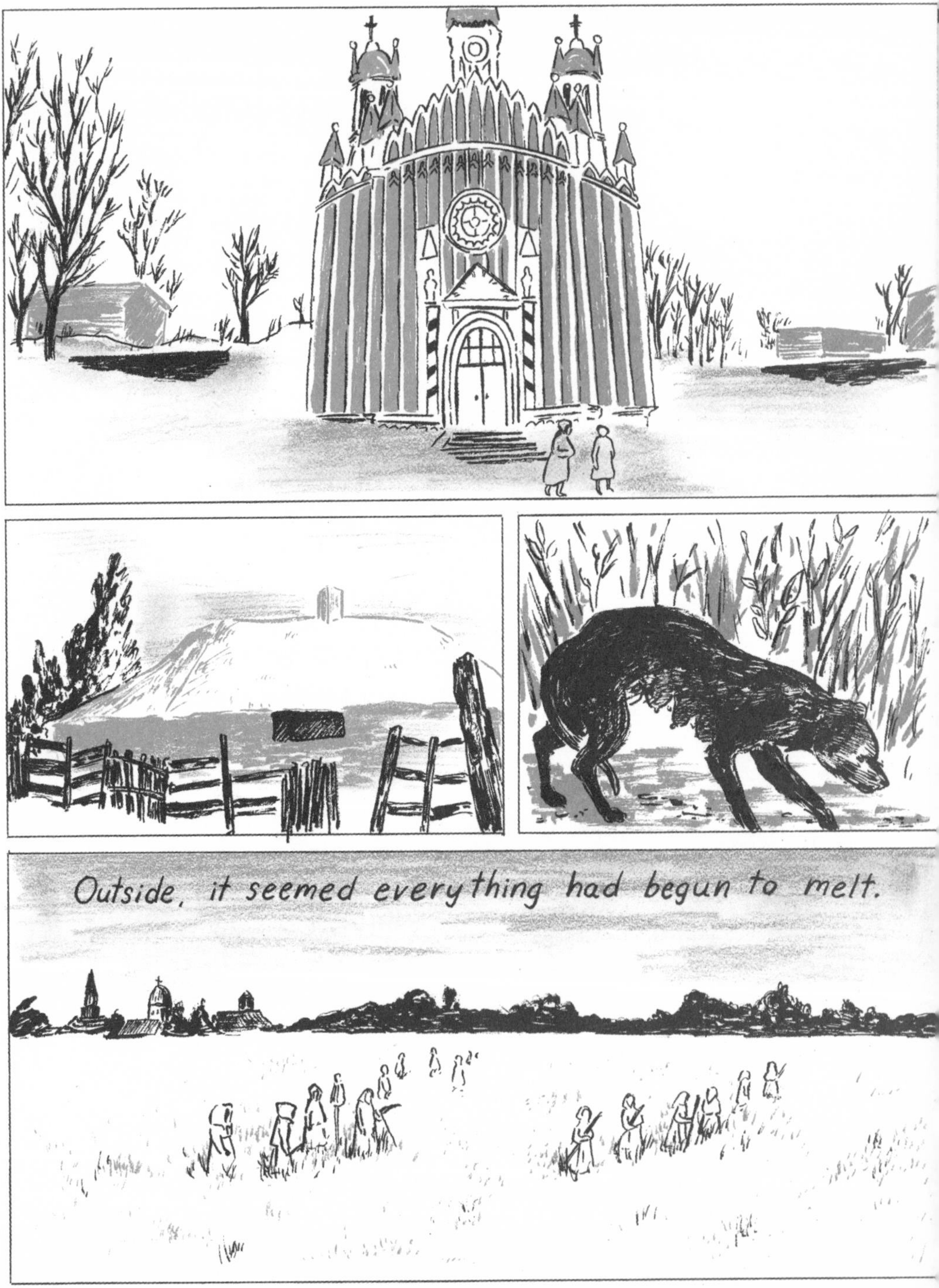
Outside, it seemed everything had begun to melt.

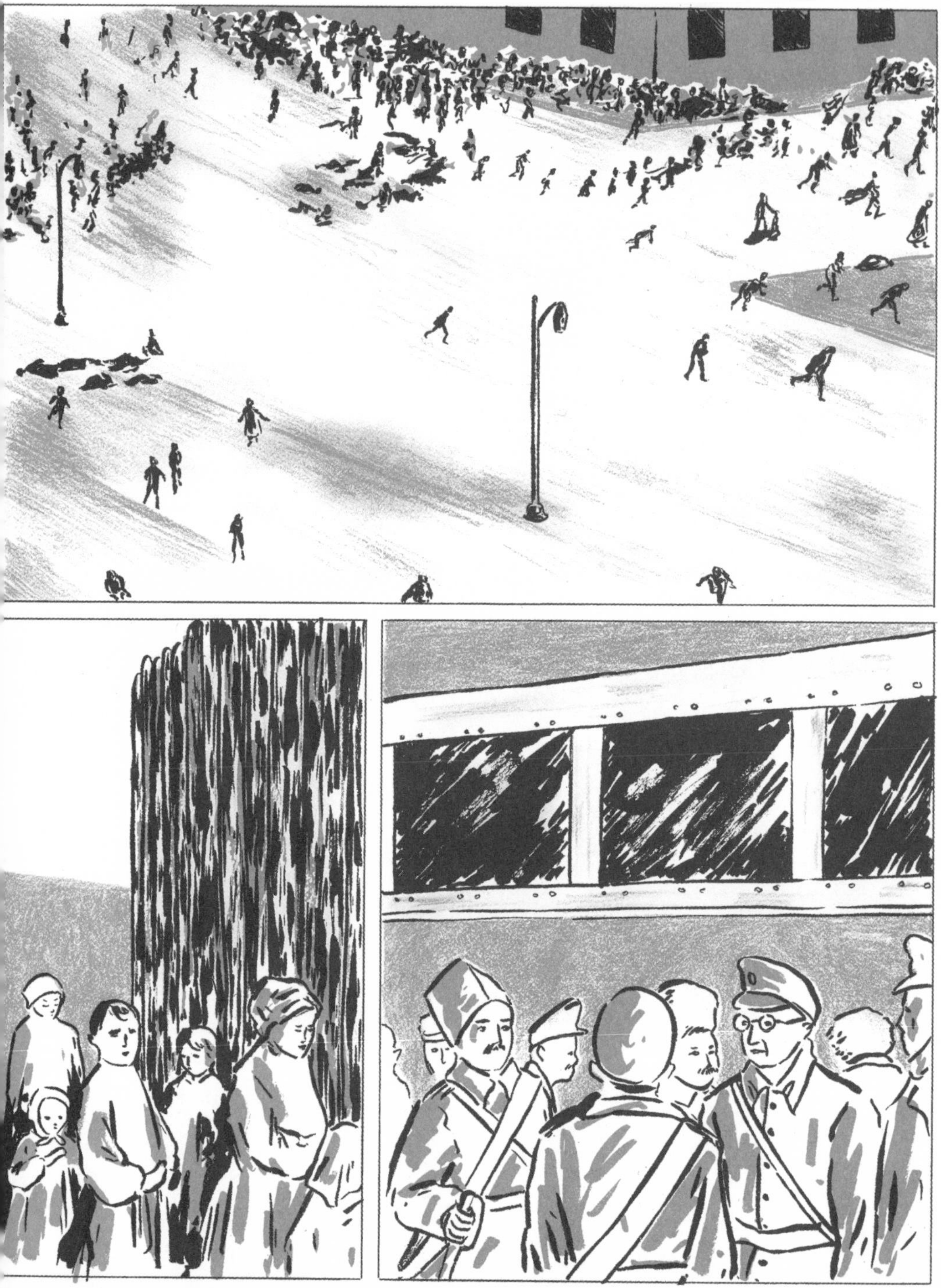

I thought often about the field from my dream. In the afternoons I would walk around the grounds, looking for a way to replicate it in a photograph,

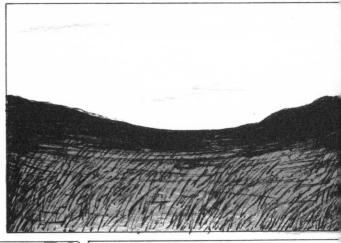

but something

was always

getting in

the way.

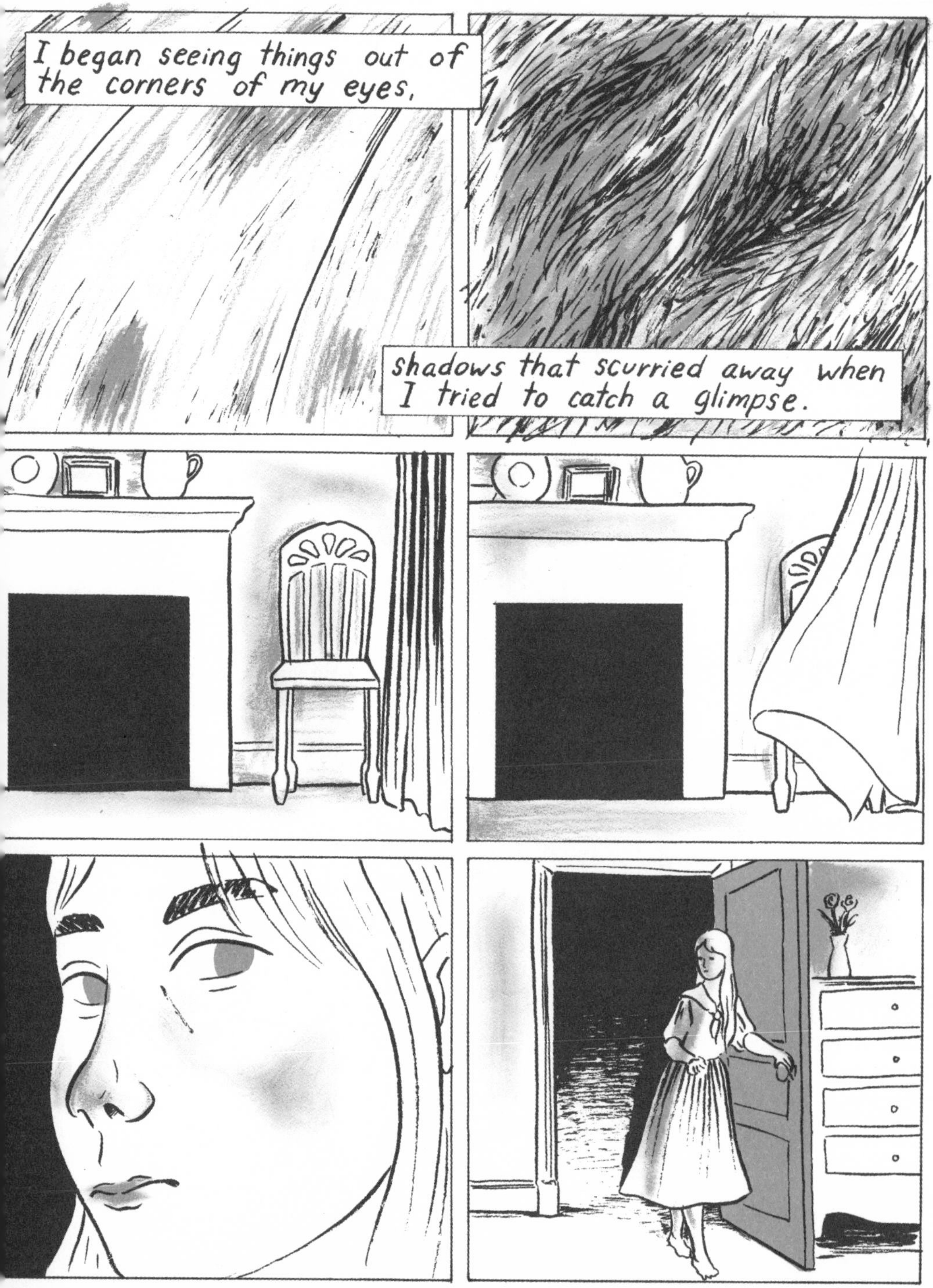
I began seeing things out of the corners of my eyes,
shadows that scurried away when I tried to catch a glimpse.

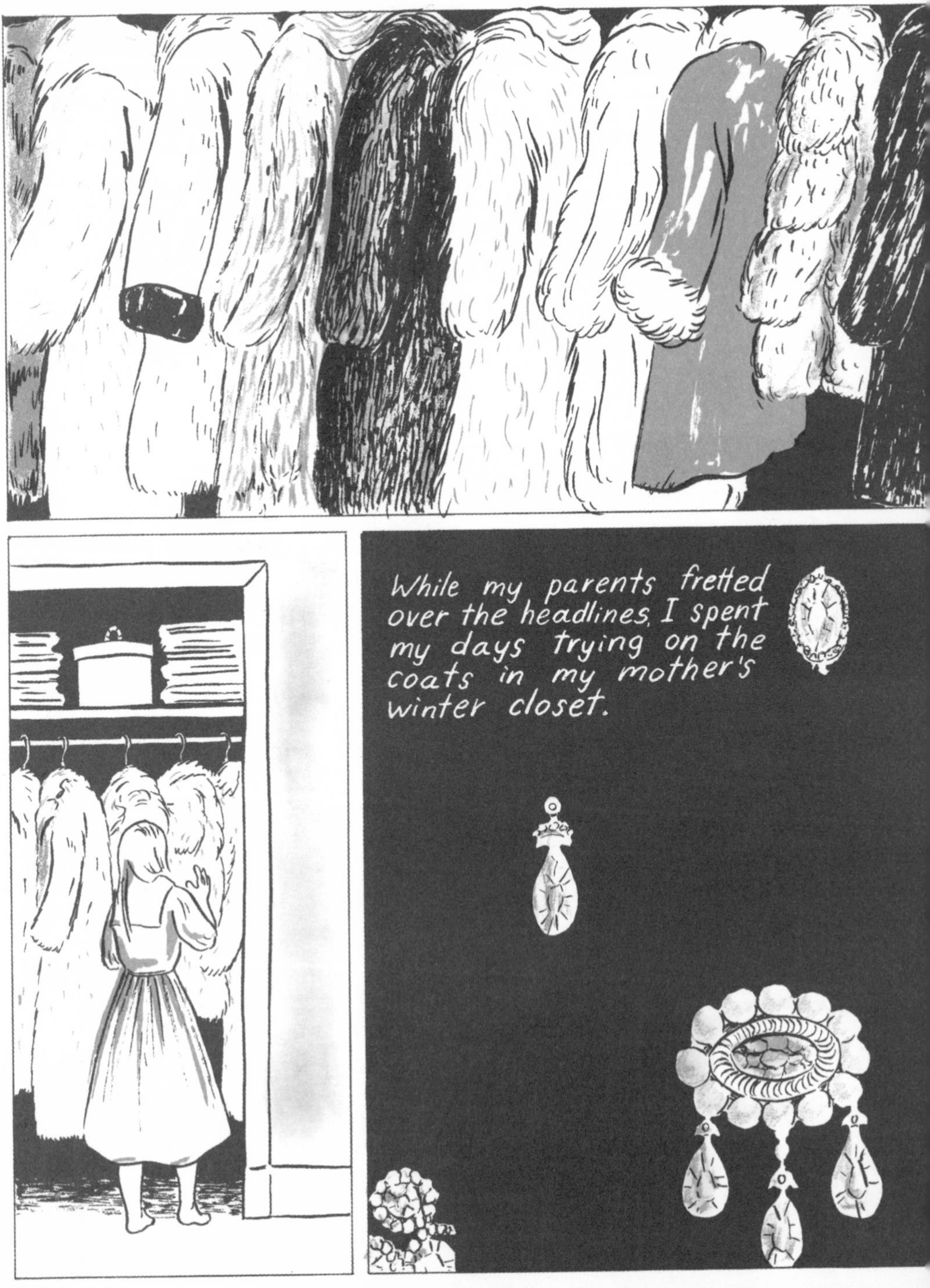
While my parents fretted over the headlines, I spent my days trying on the coats in my mother's winter closet.

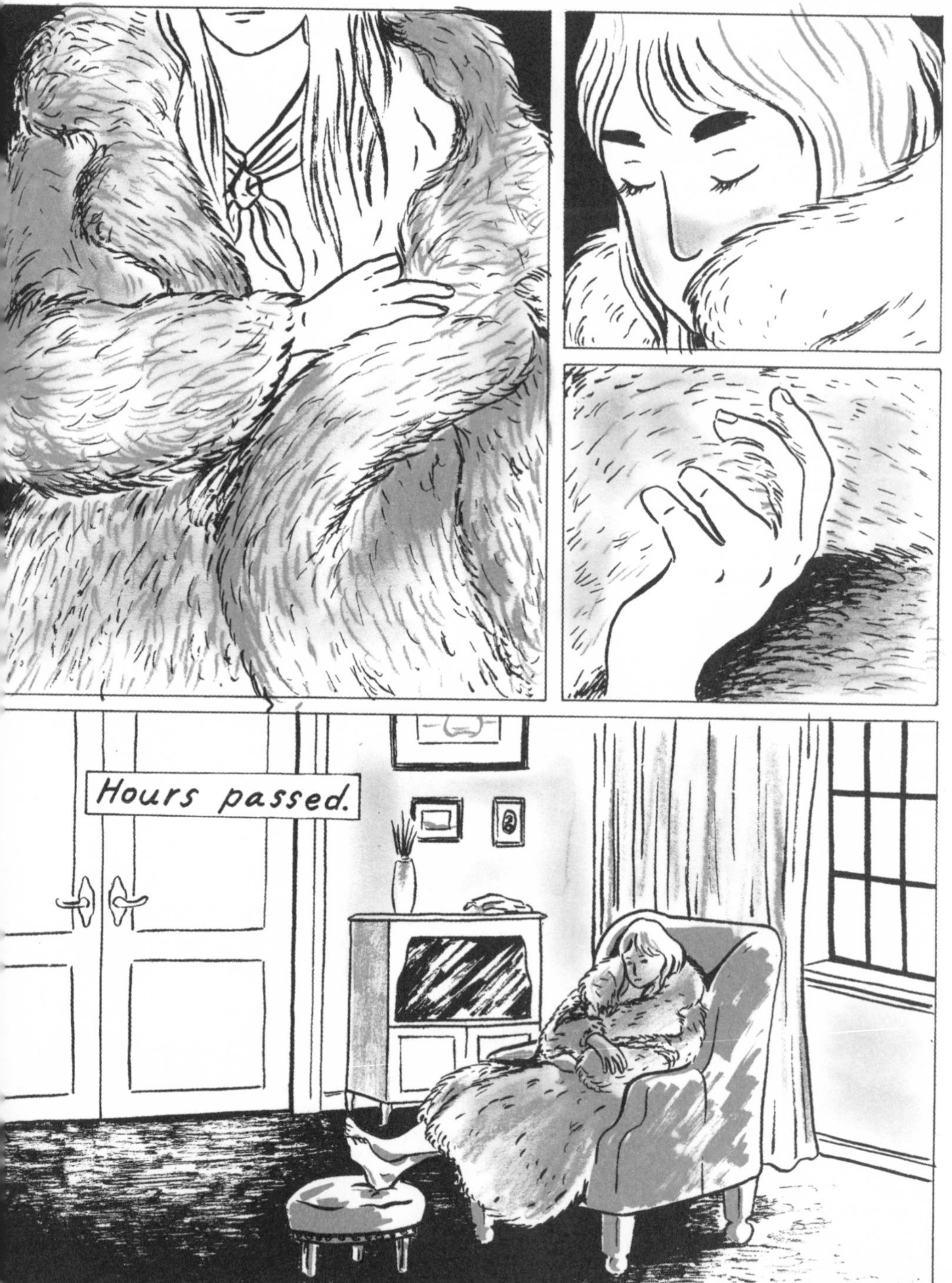
Hours passed.

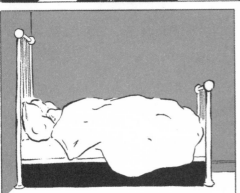

Most nights, I returned to the field in my dreams.

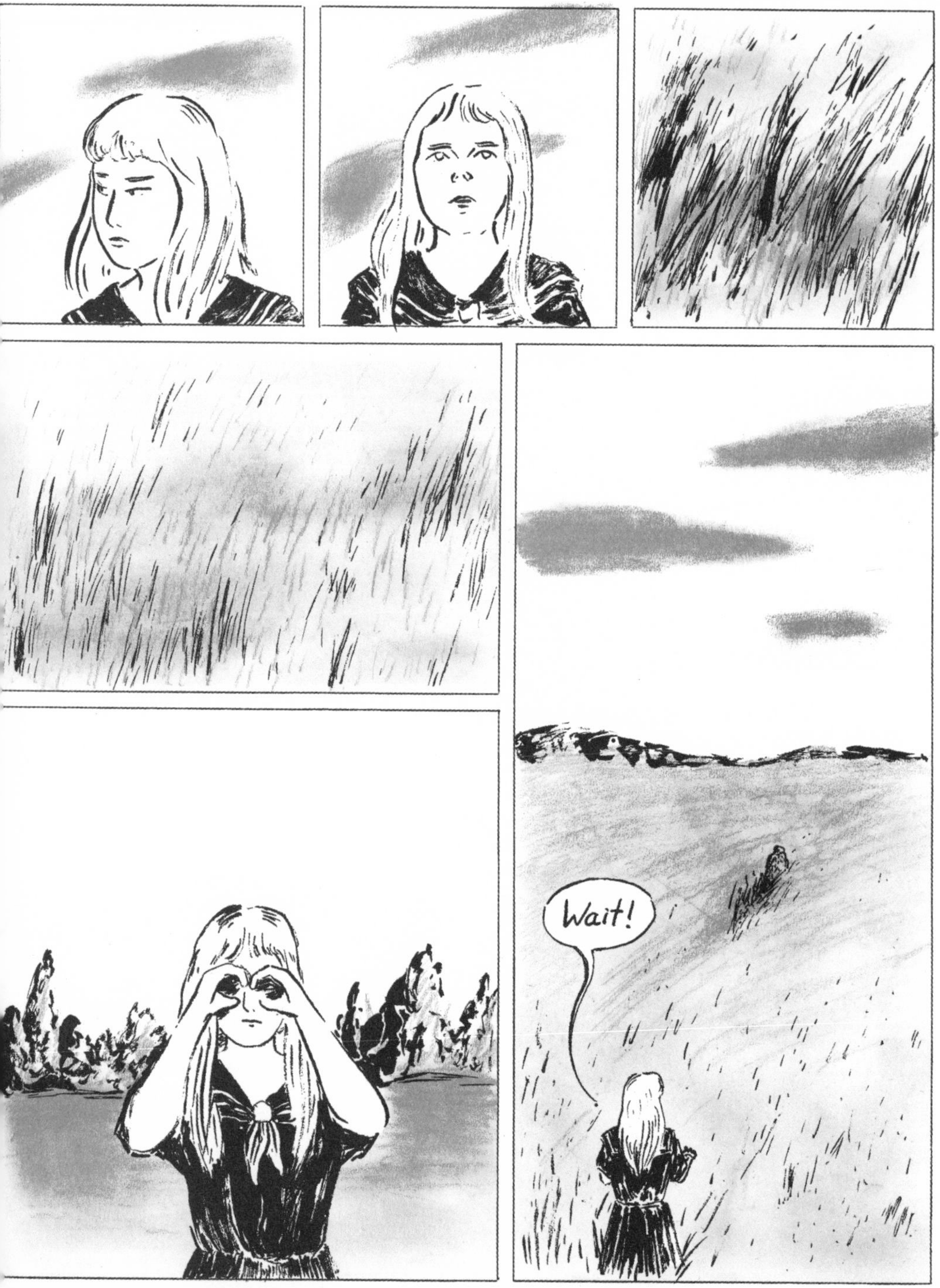
Wait!

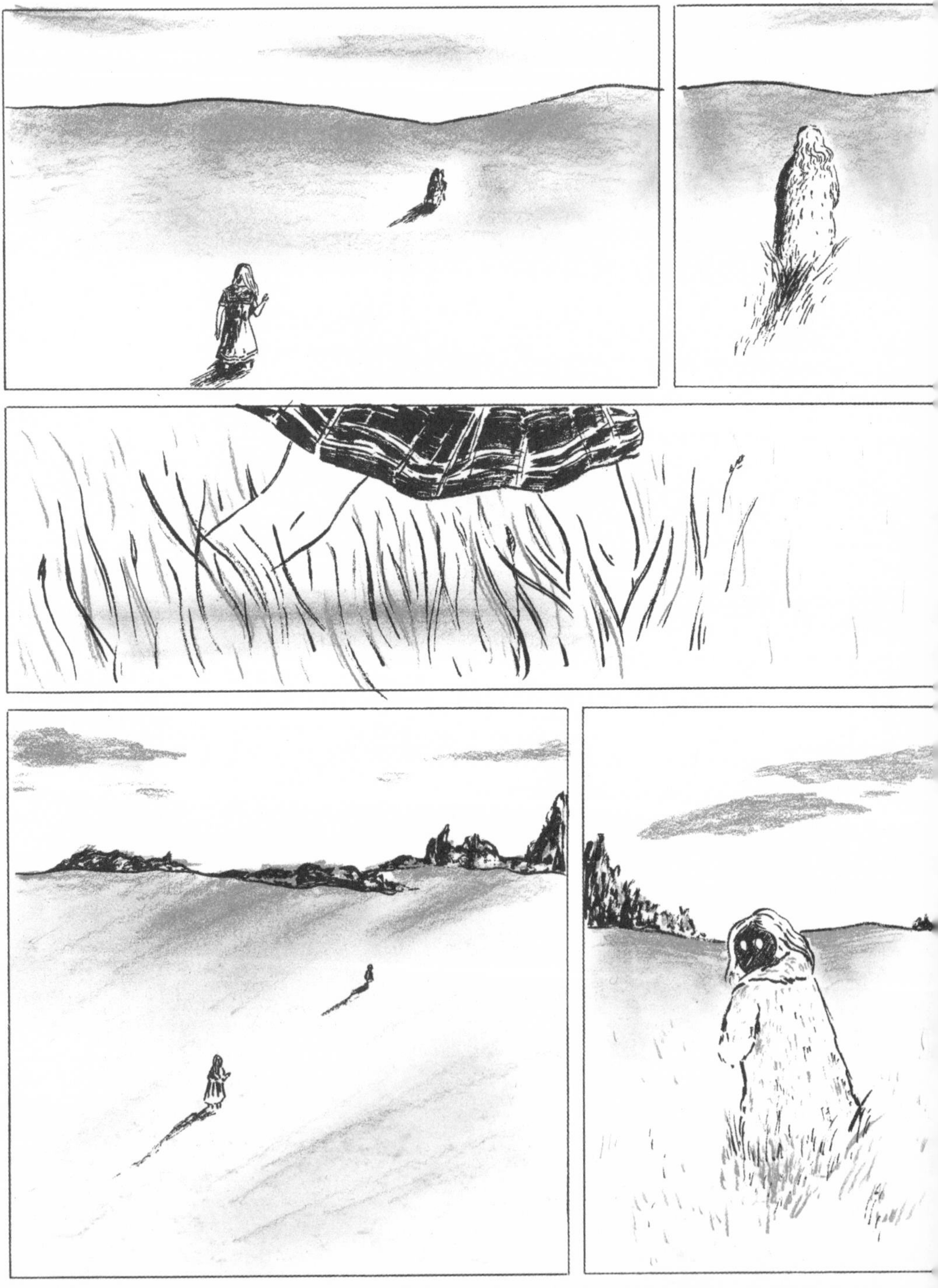

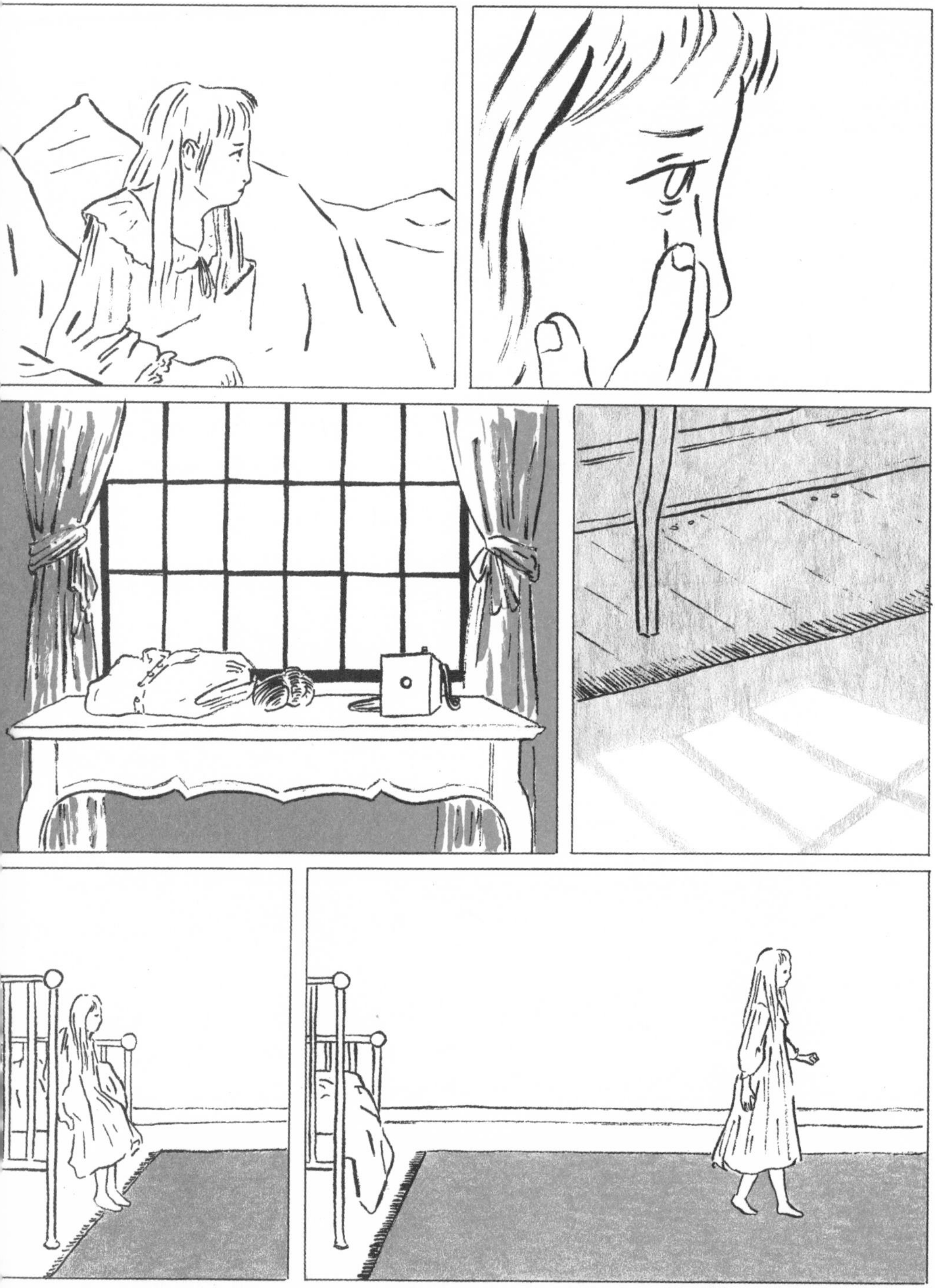

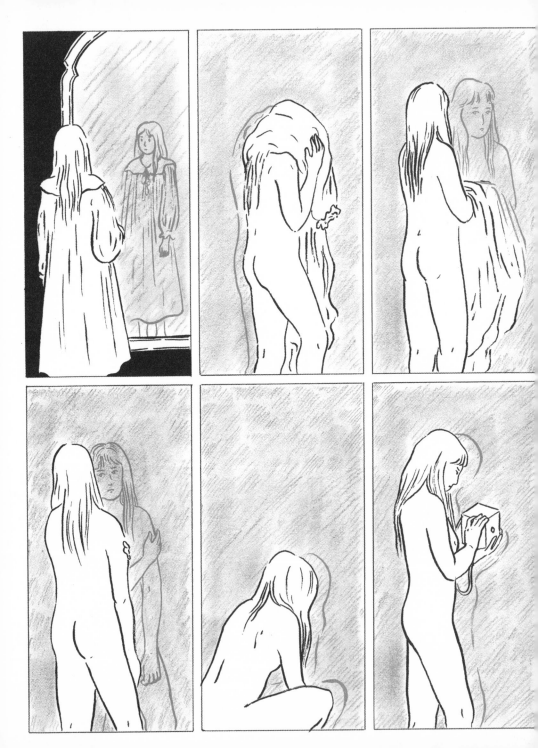

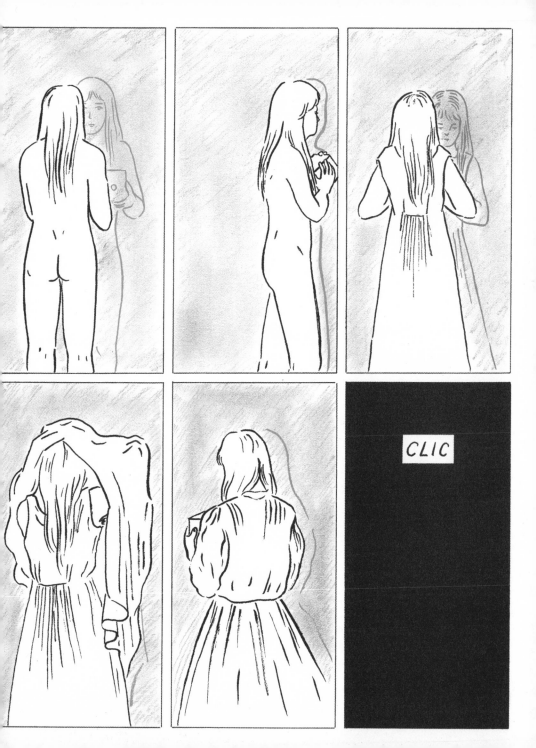

CLIC

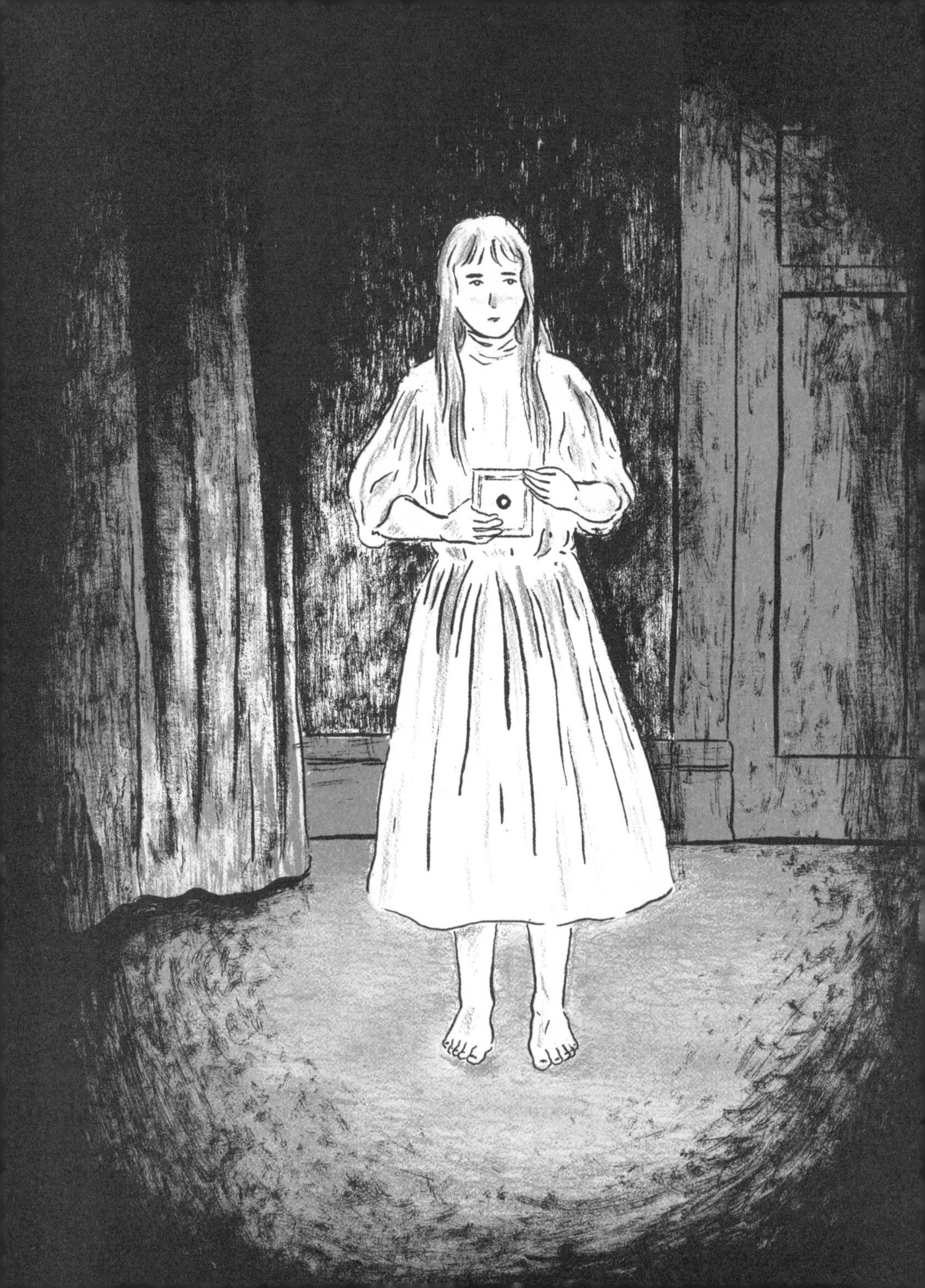

Anastasia, come lend us a hand.

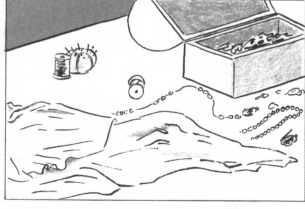

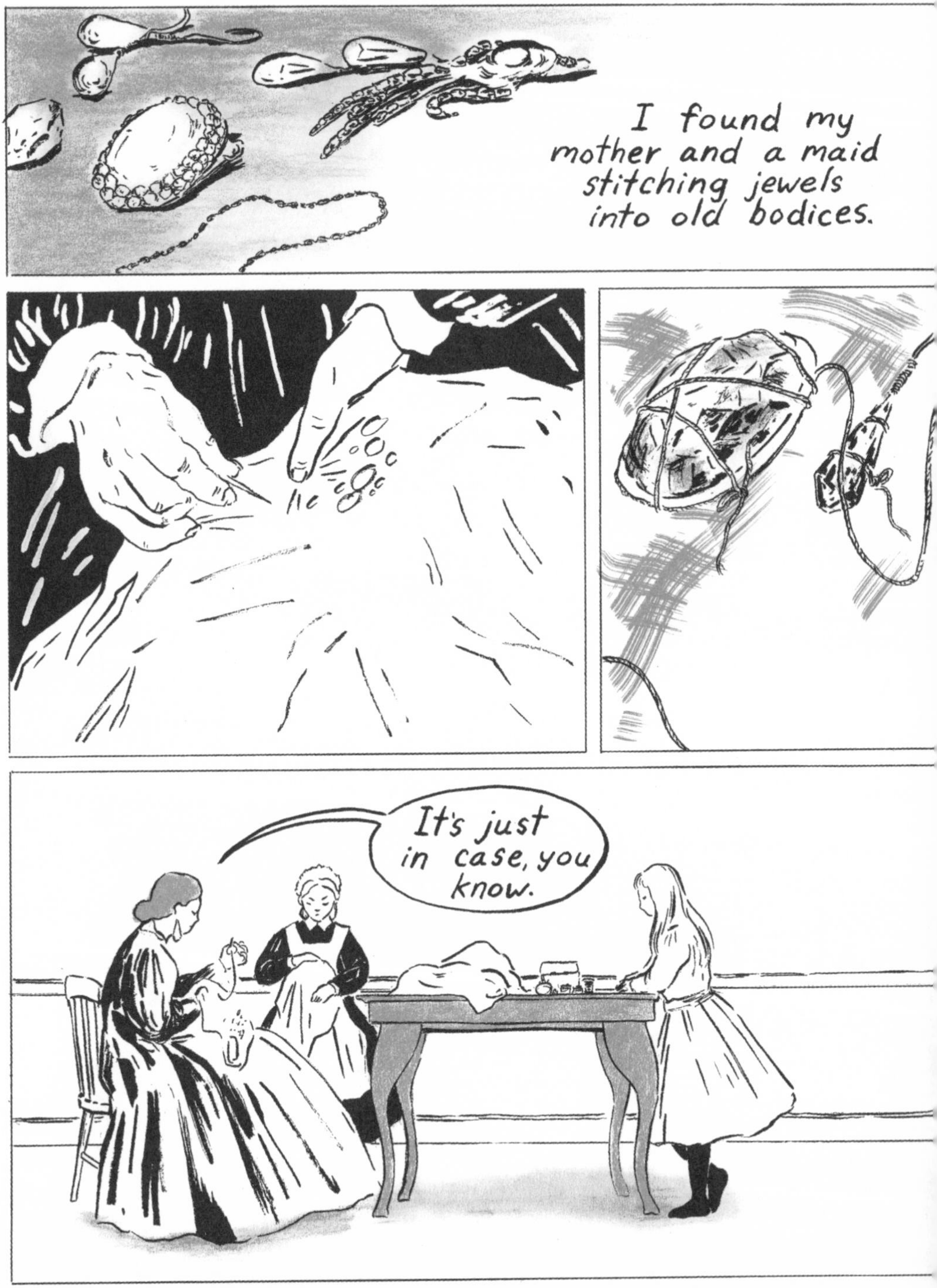
I found my mother and a maid stitching jewels into old bodices.
It's just in case, you know.

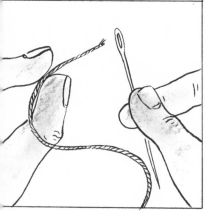

this one is finished, your highness.

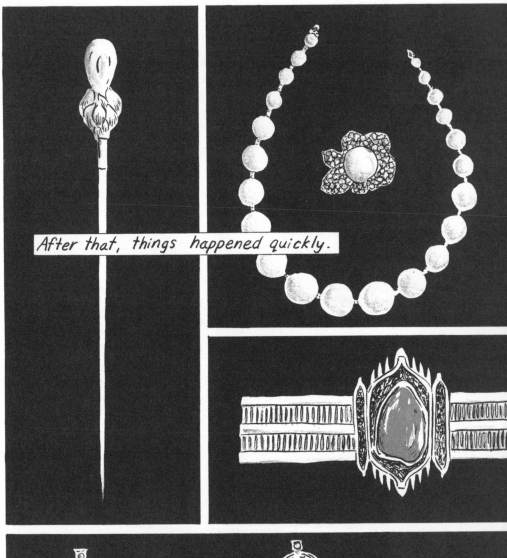

After that, things happened quickly.

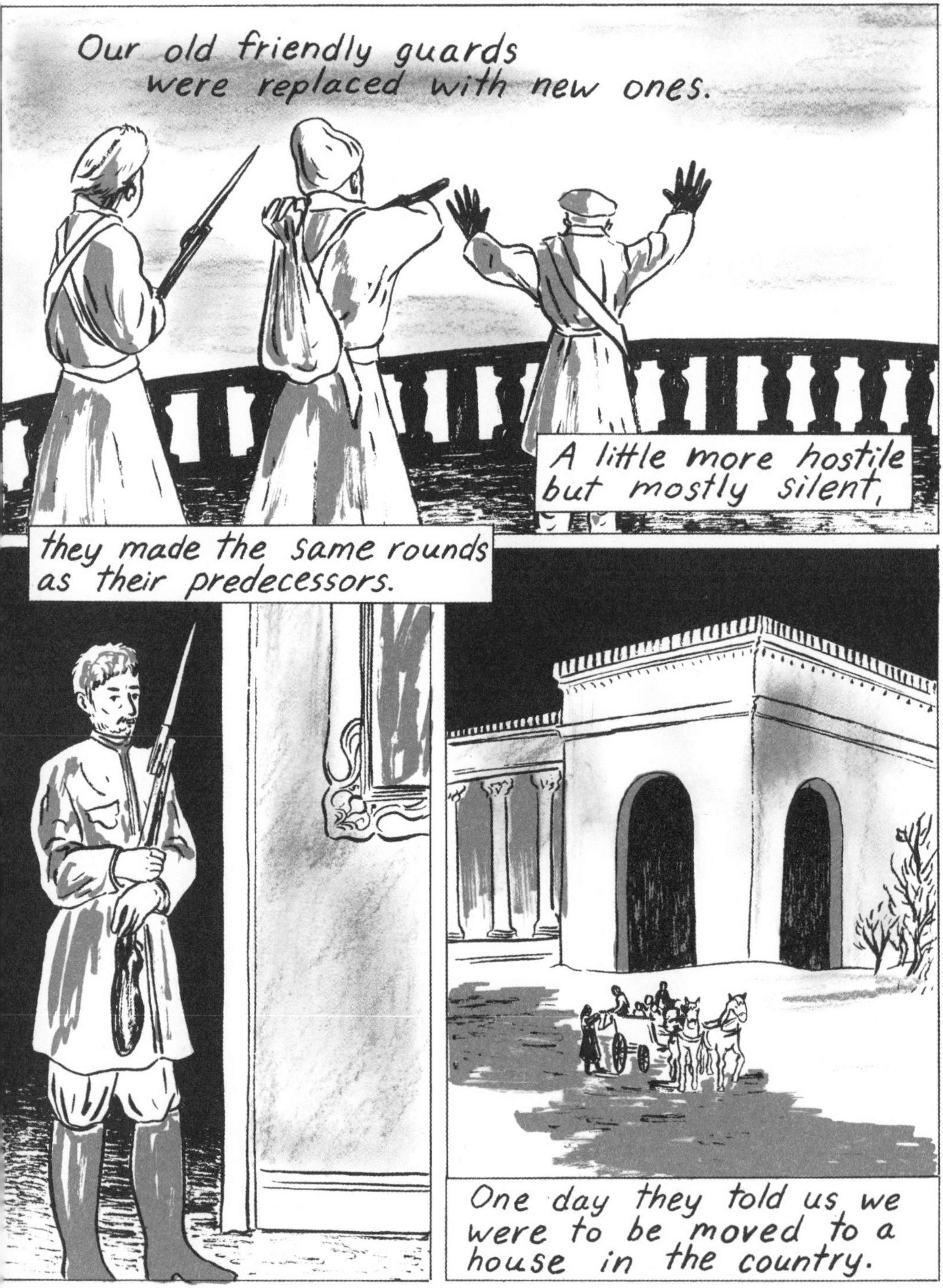
Our old friendly guards were replaced with new ones.
A little more hostile but mostly silent,
they made the same rounds as their predecessors.
One day they told us we were to be moved to a house in the country.

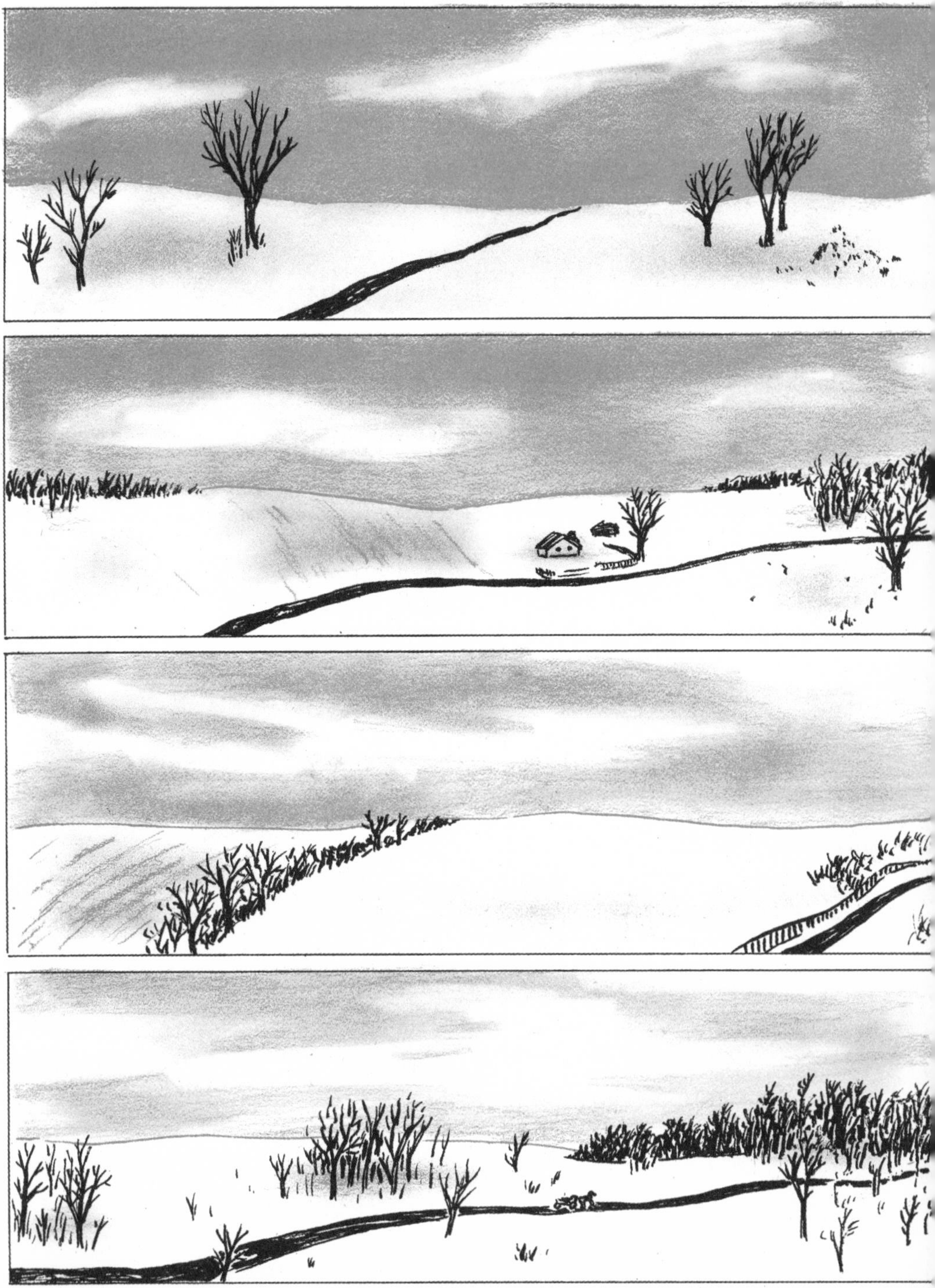

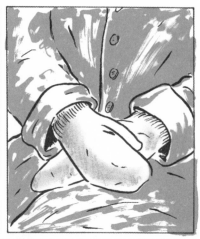

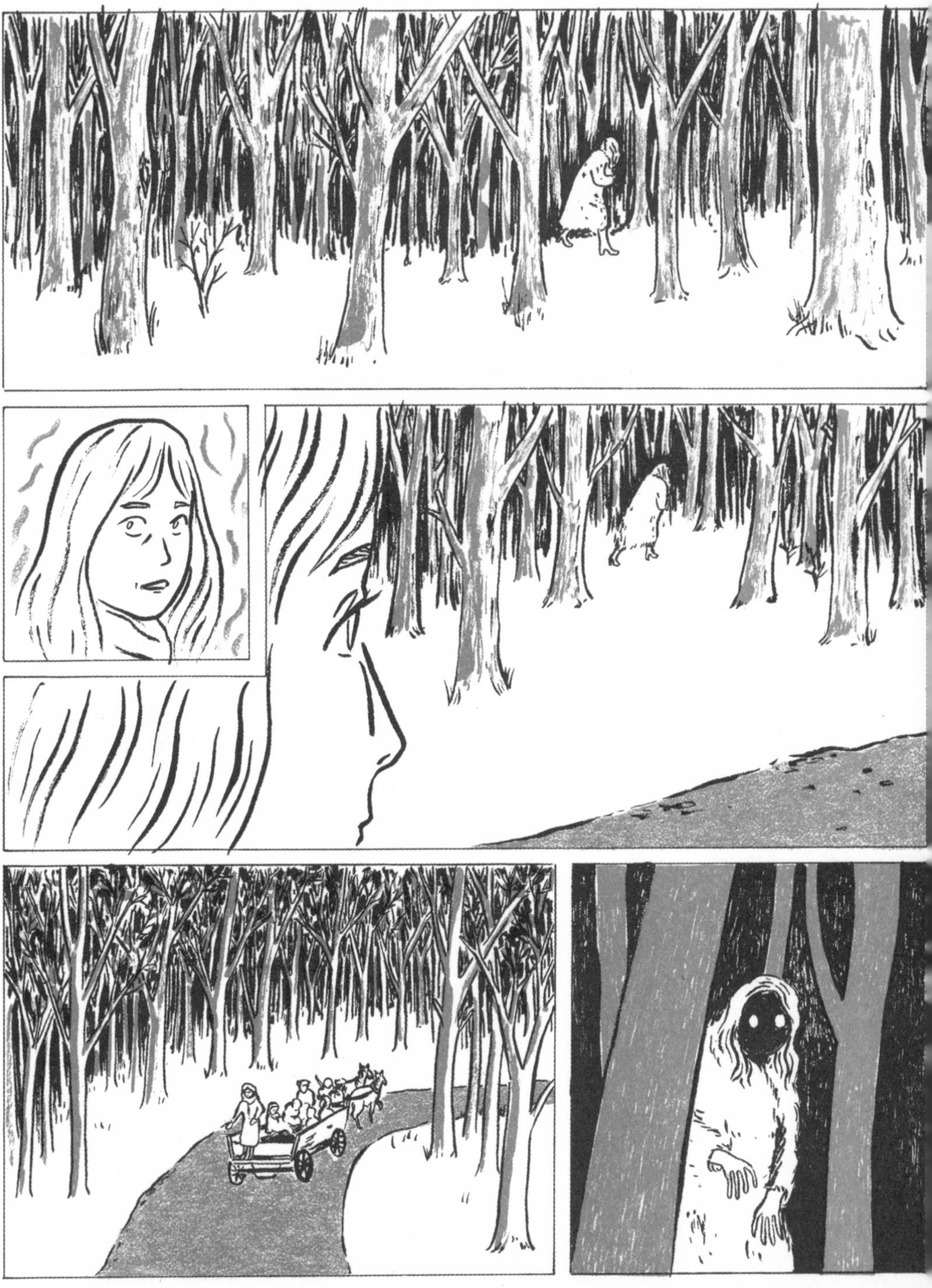

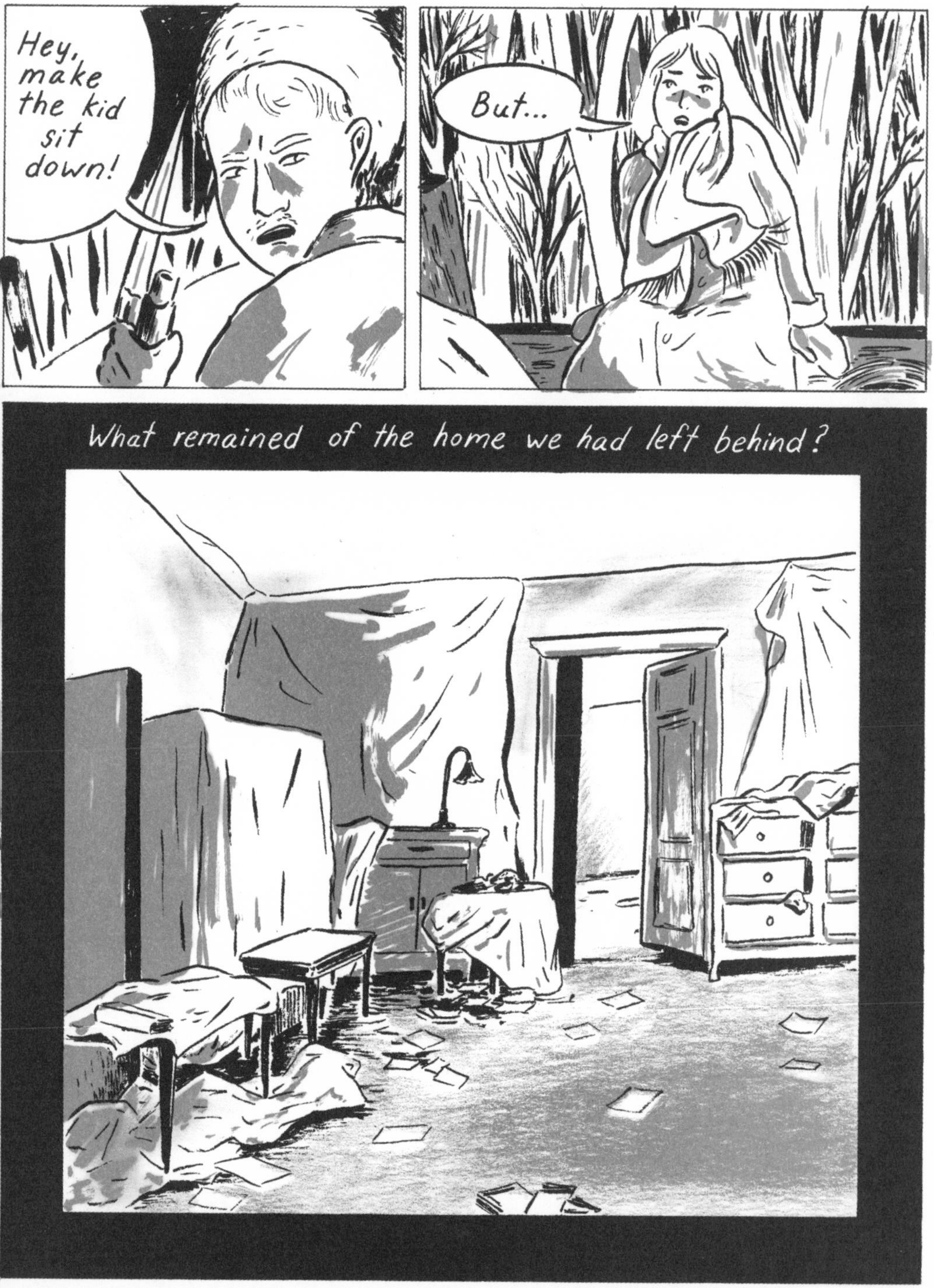
Hey, make the kid sit down!
But...
What remained of the home we had left behind?

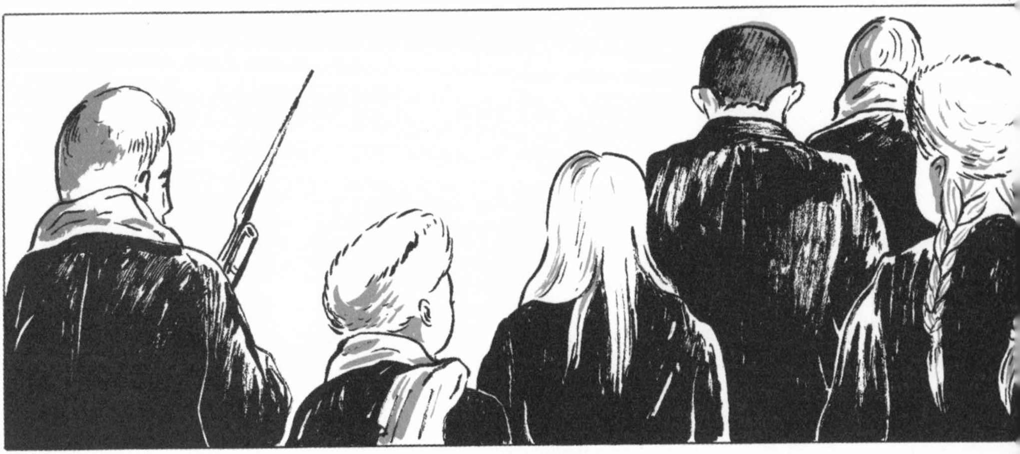
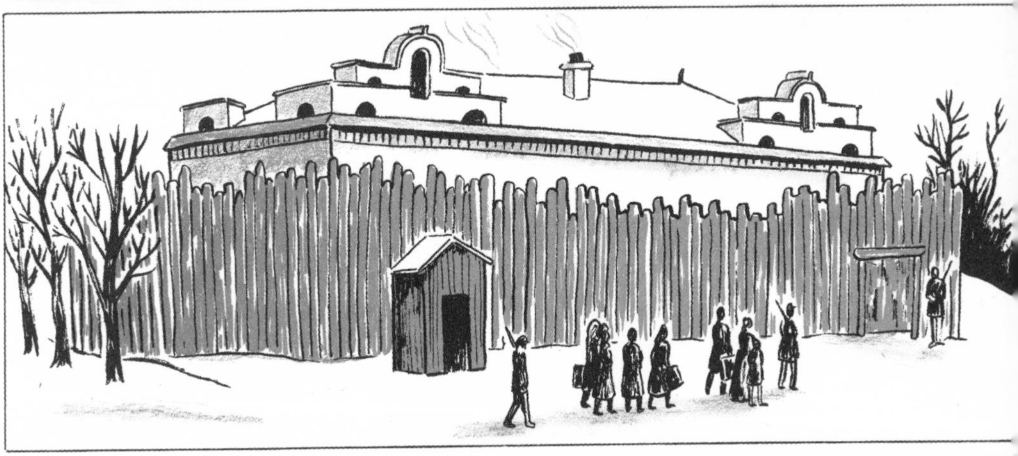
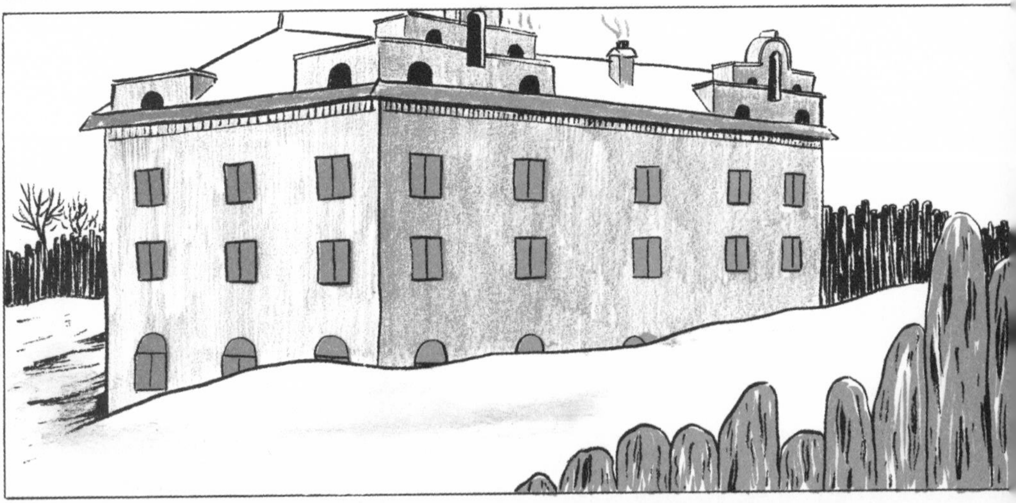

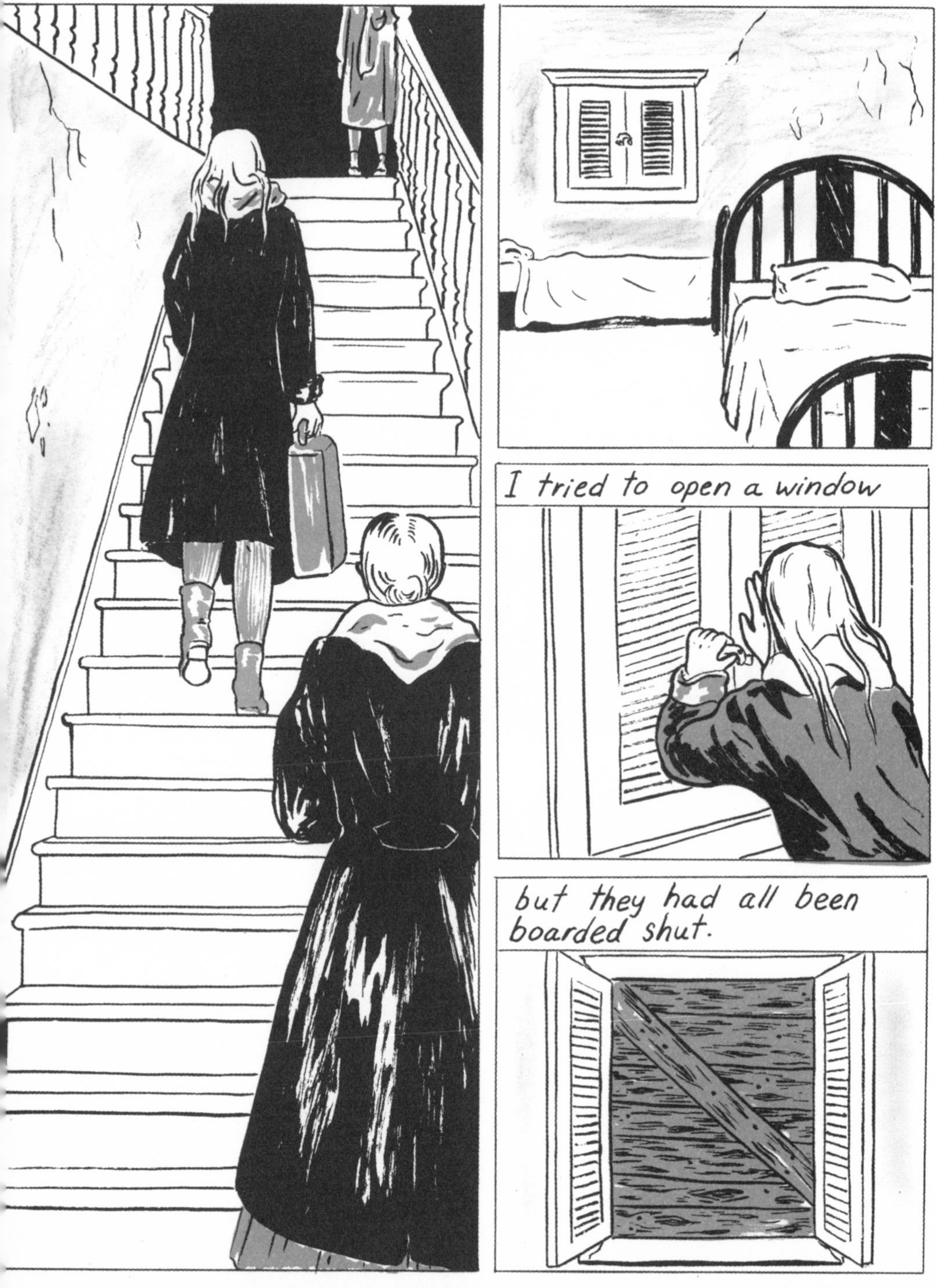
I tried to open a window
but they had all been boarded shut.

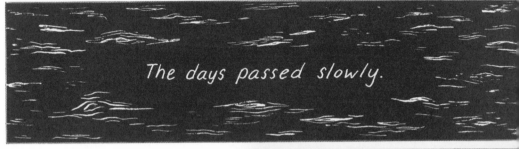

The days passed slowly.

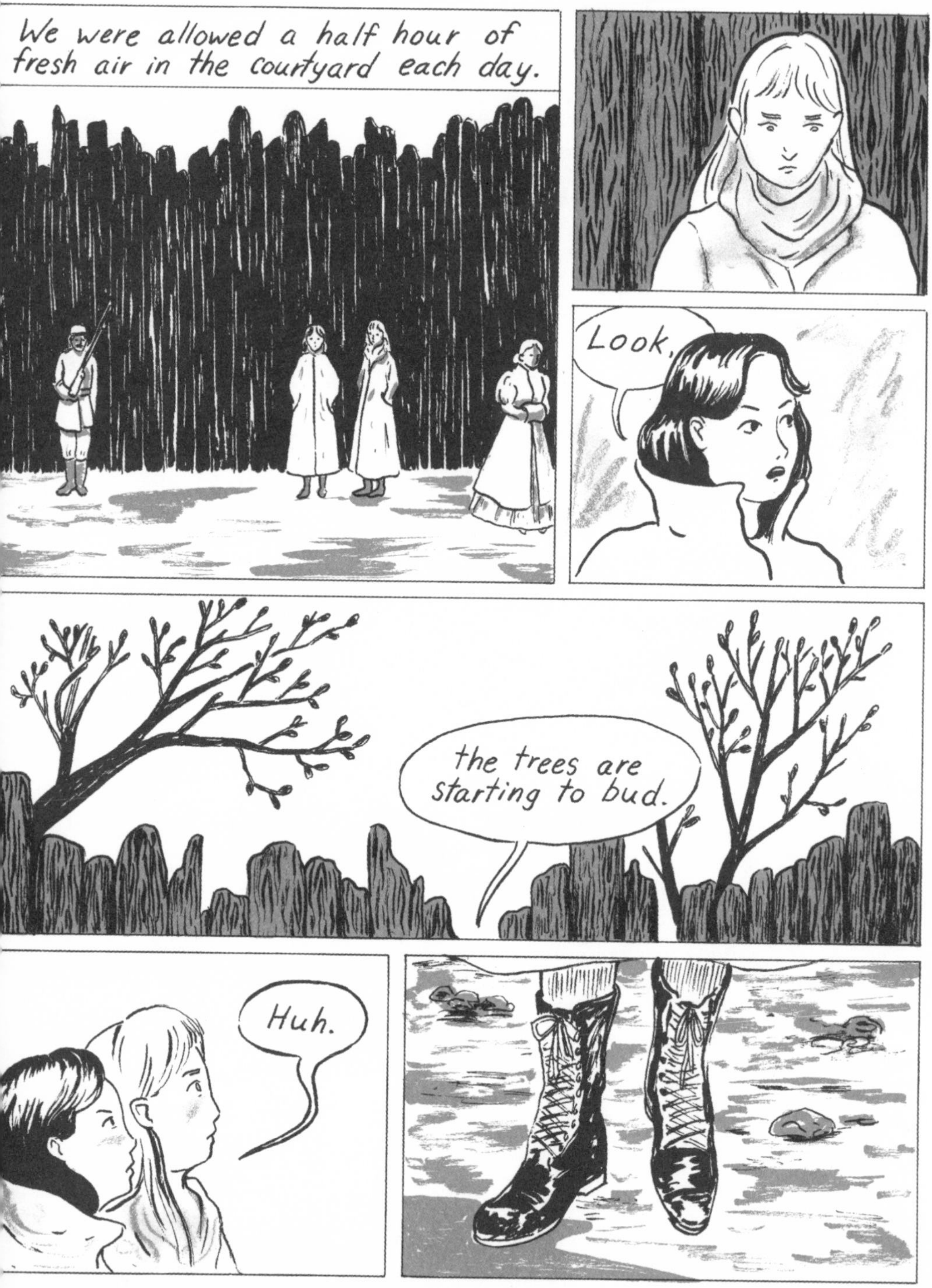
We were allowed a half hour of fresh air in the courtyard each day.
Look,
the trees are starting to bud.
Huh.

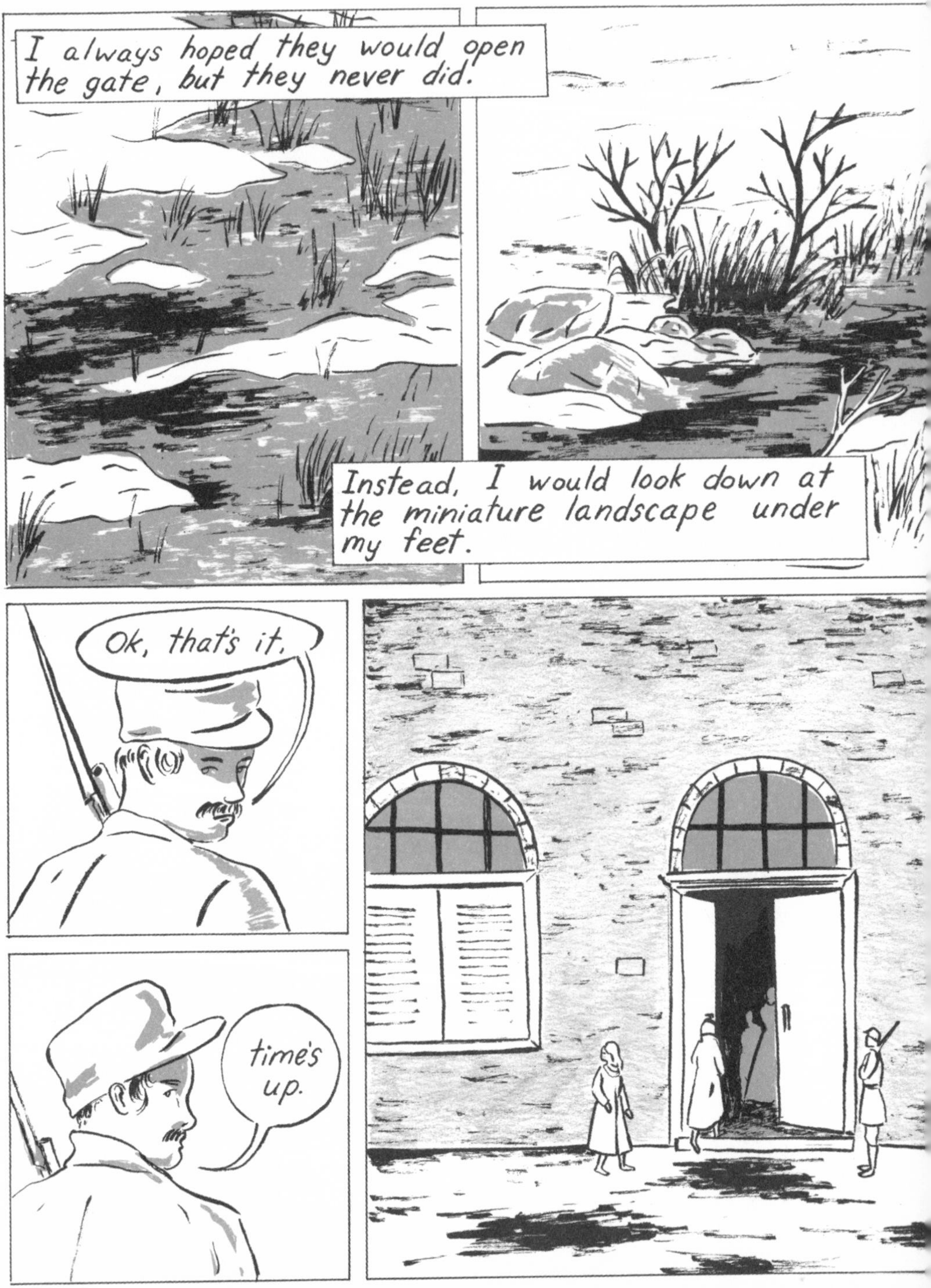
I always hoped they would open the gate, but they never did.
Instead, I would look down at the miniature landscape under my feet.
Ok, that's it.
time's up.

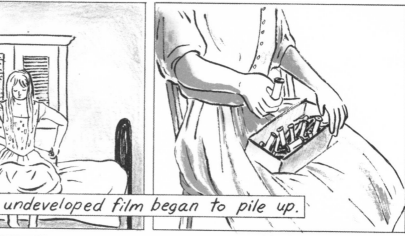

My rolls of undeveloped film began to pile up.

I tried to imagine the pictures they would become.

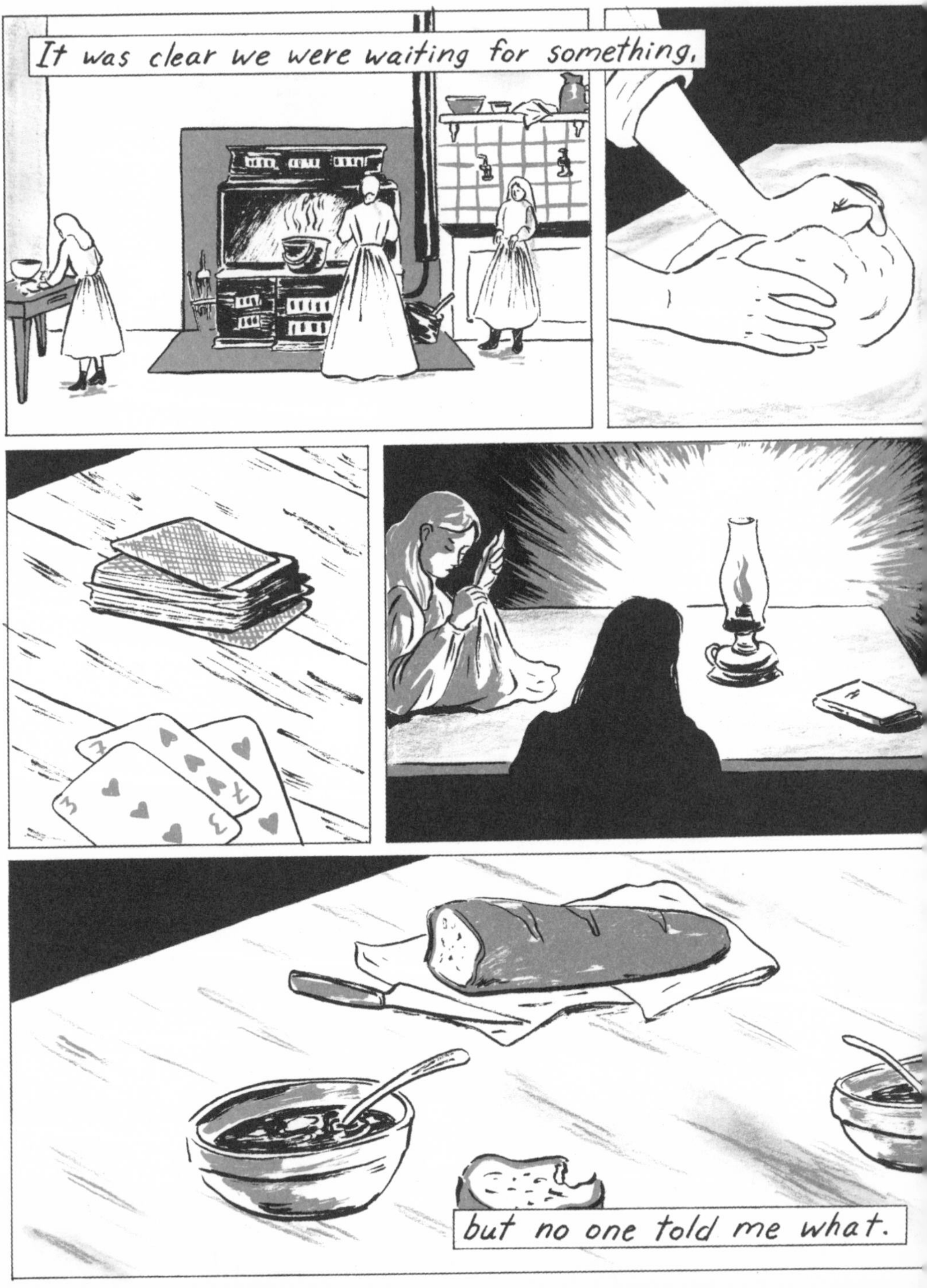
It was clear we were waiting for something,
but no one told me what.

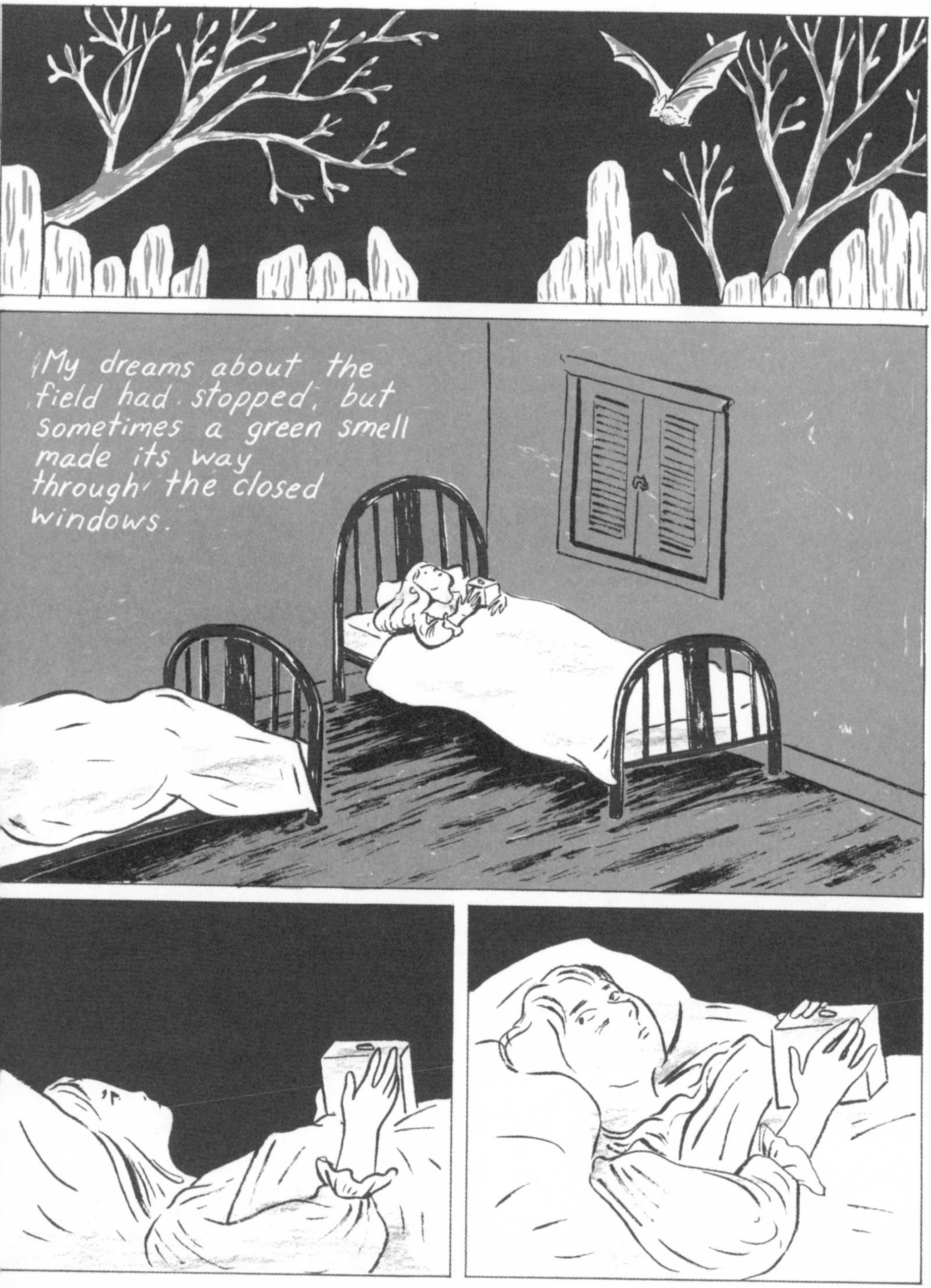
My dreams about the field had stopped, but sometimes a green smell made its way through the closed windows.

Get up.

We were given ten minutes to dress and pack.

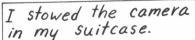

I stowed the camera in my suitcase.

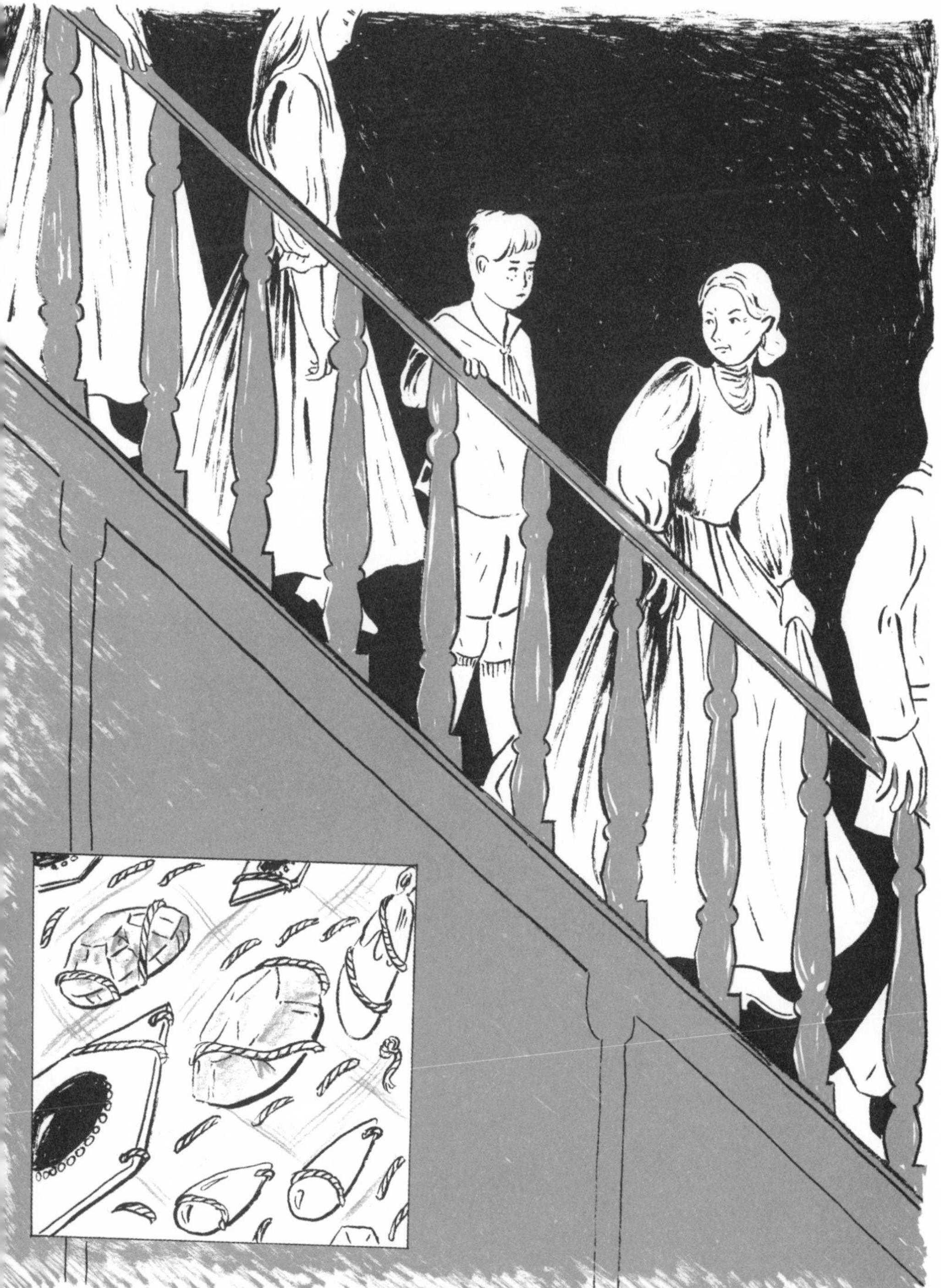

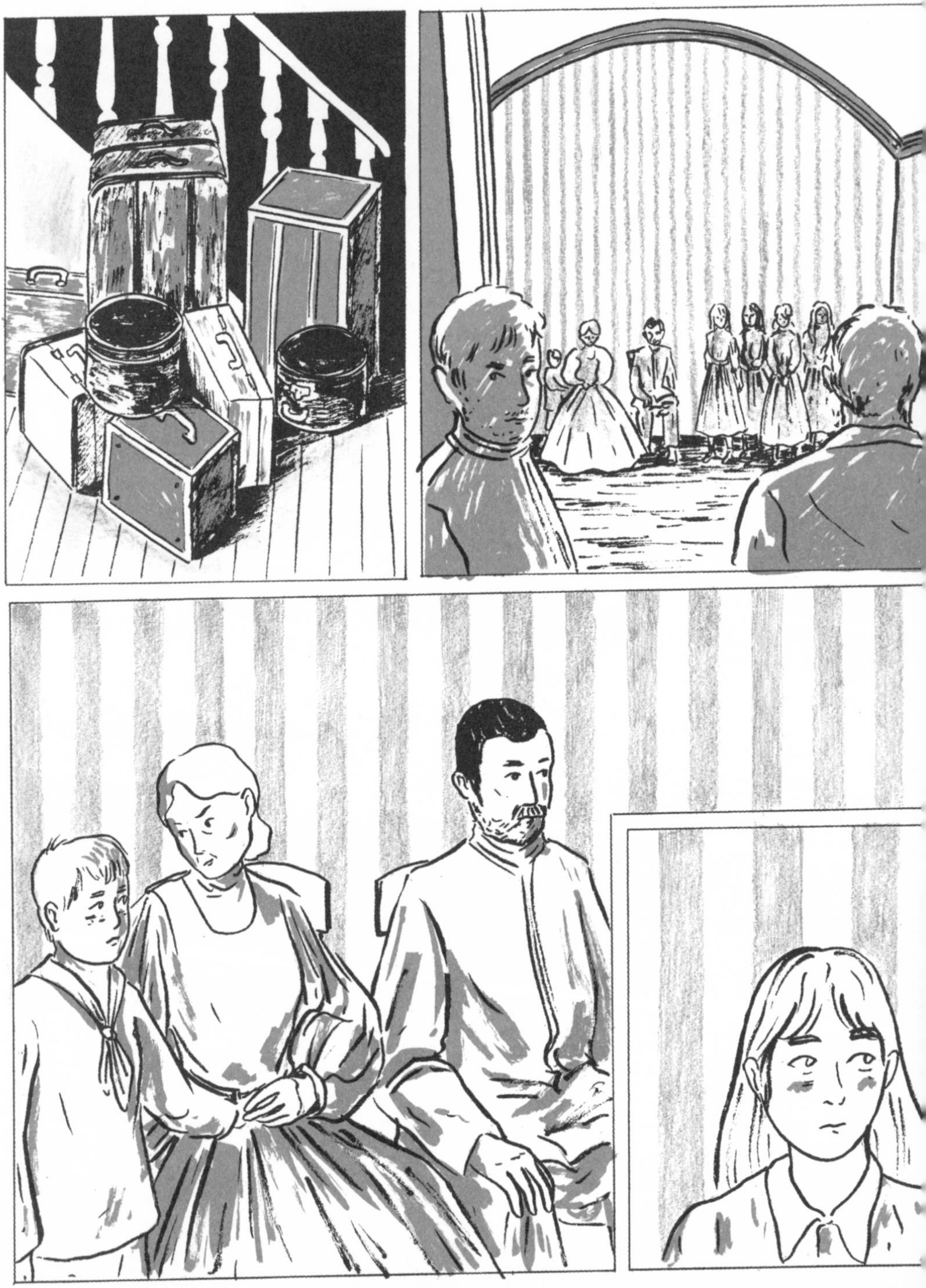

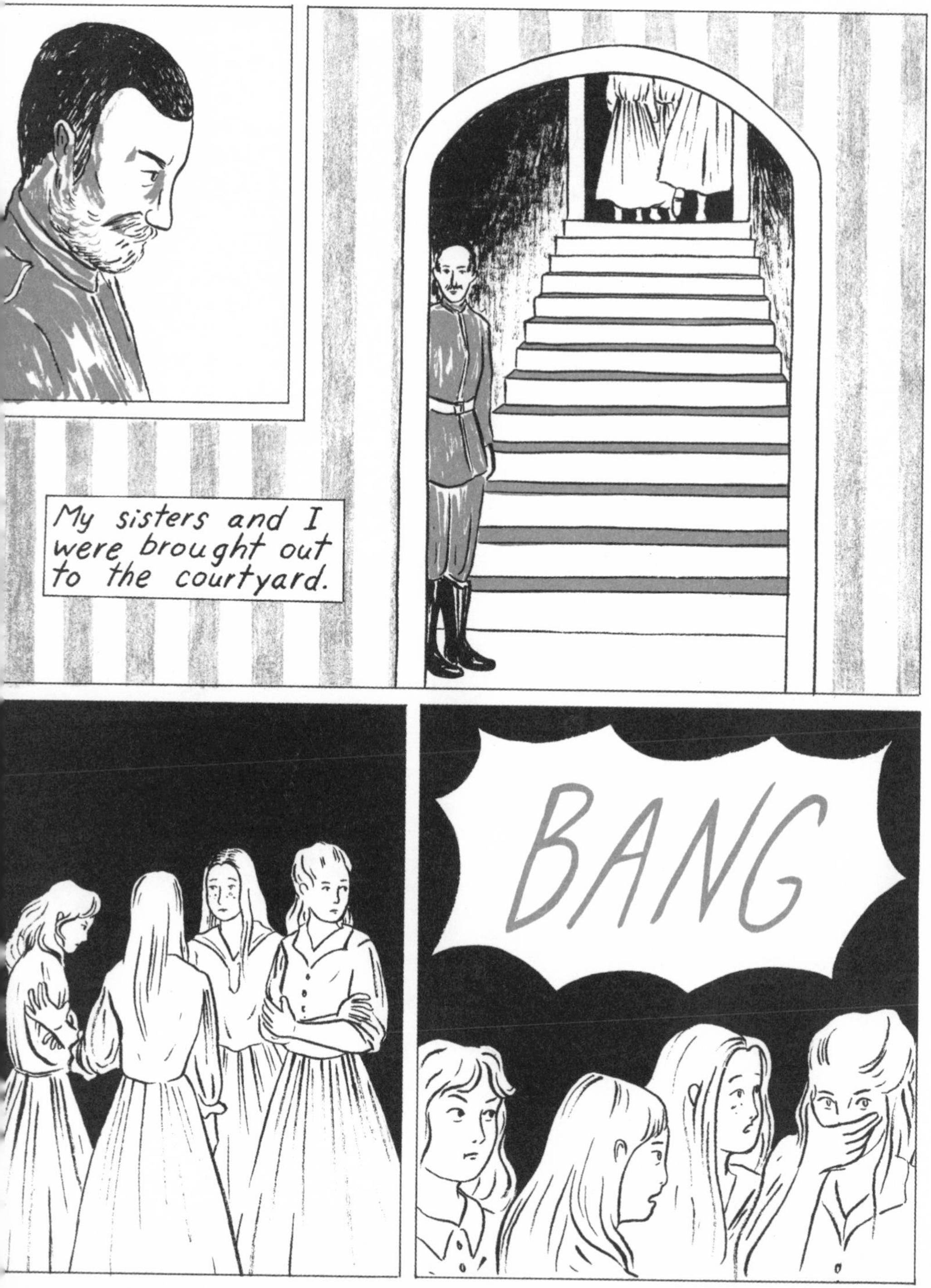
My sisters and I were brought out to the courtyard.
BANG

We'll need the two older ones.

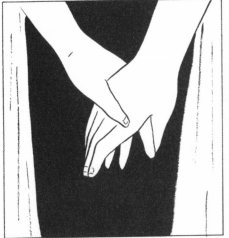

BANG

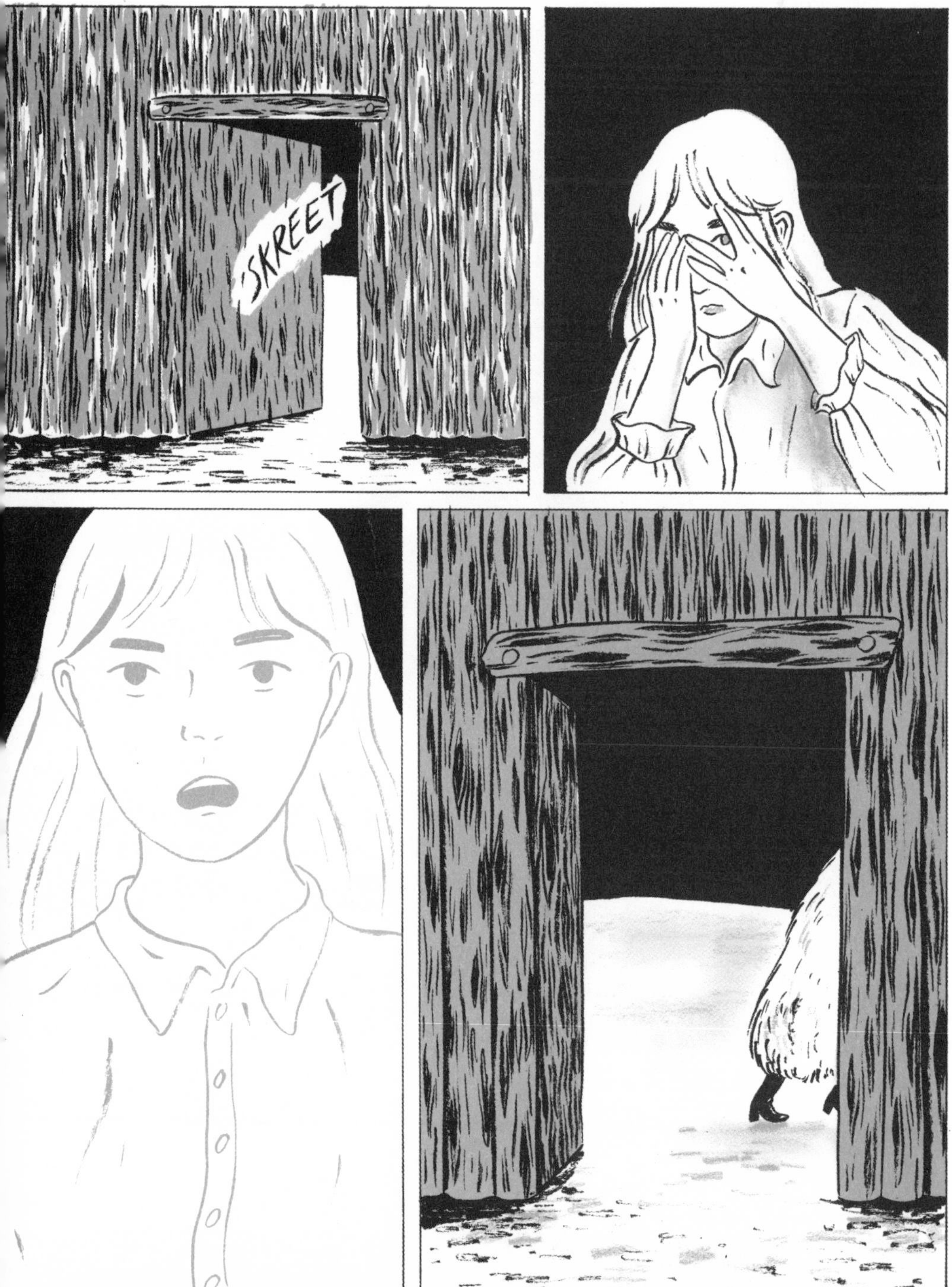
SKREET

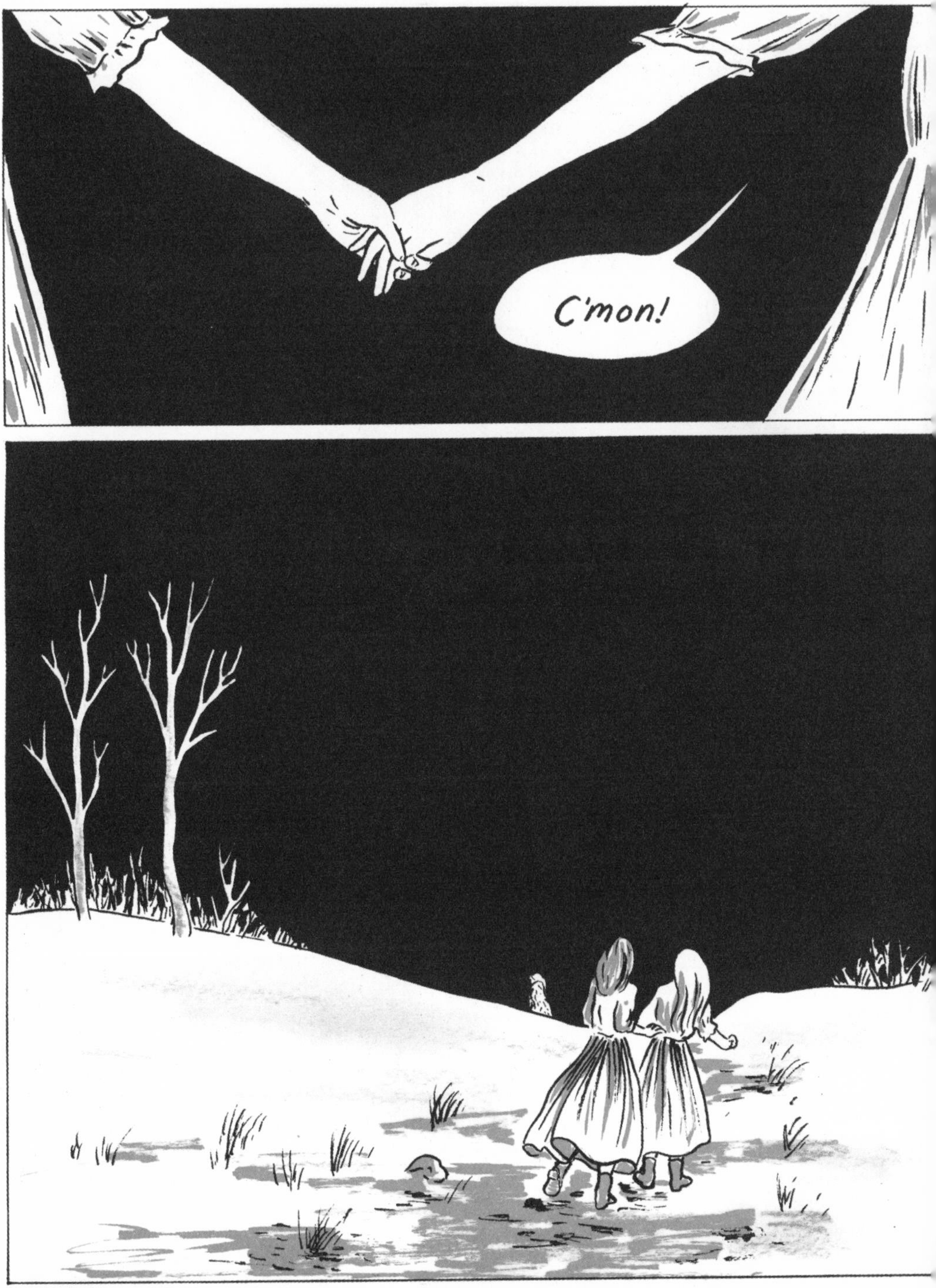
C'mon!

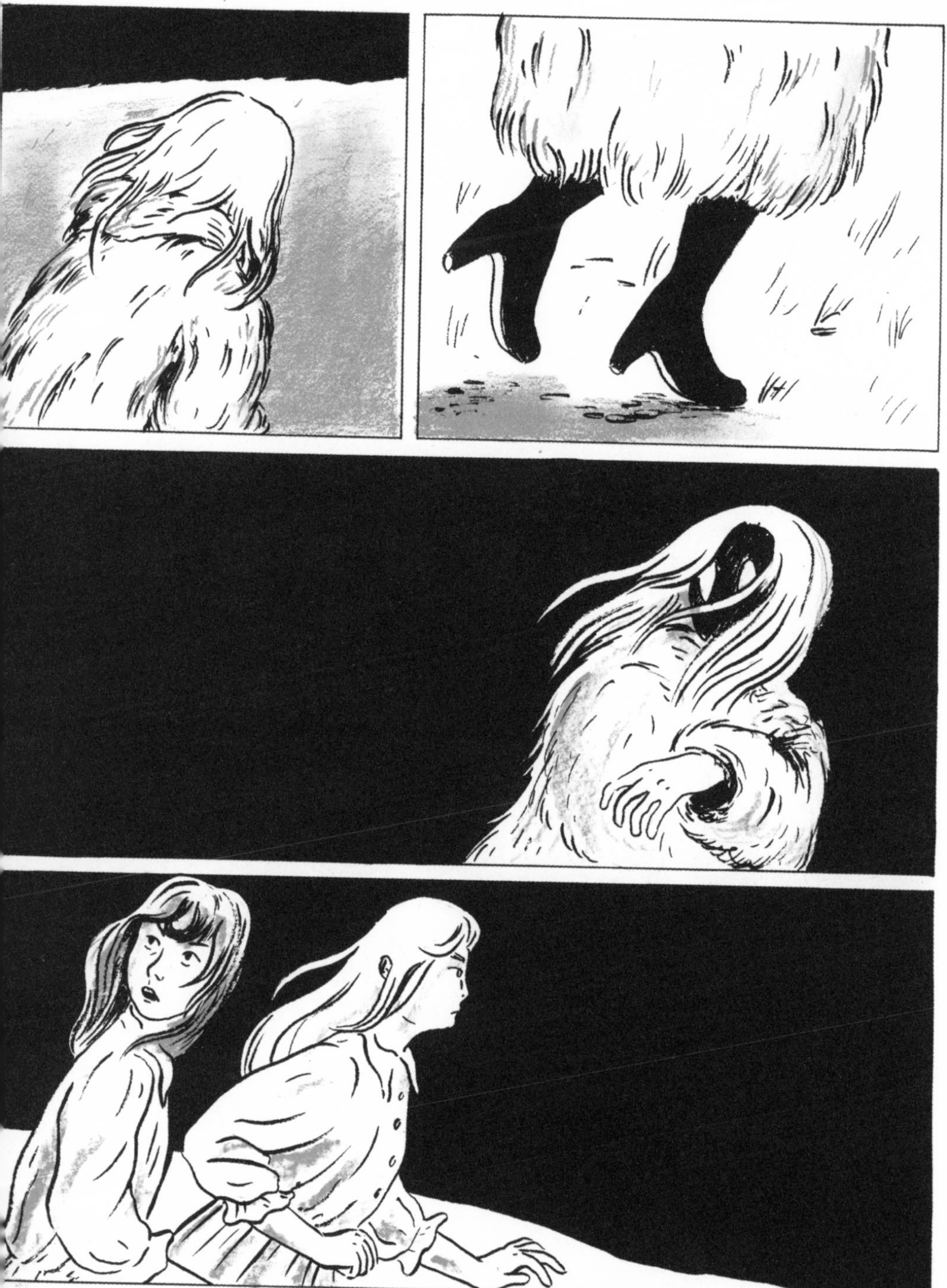

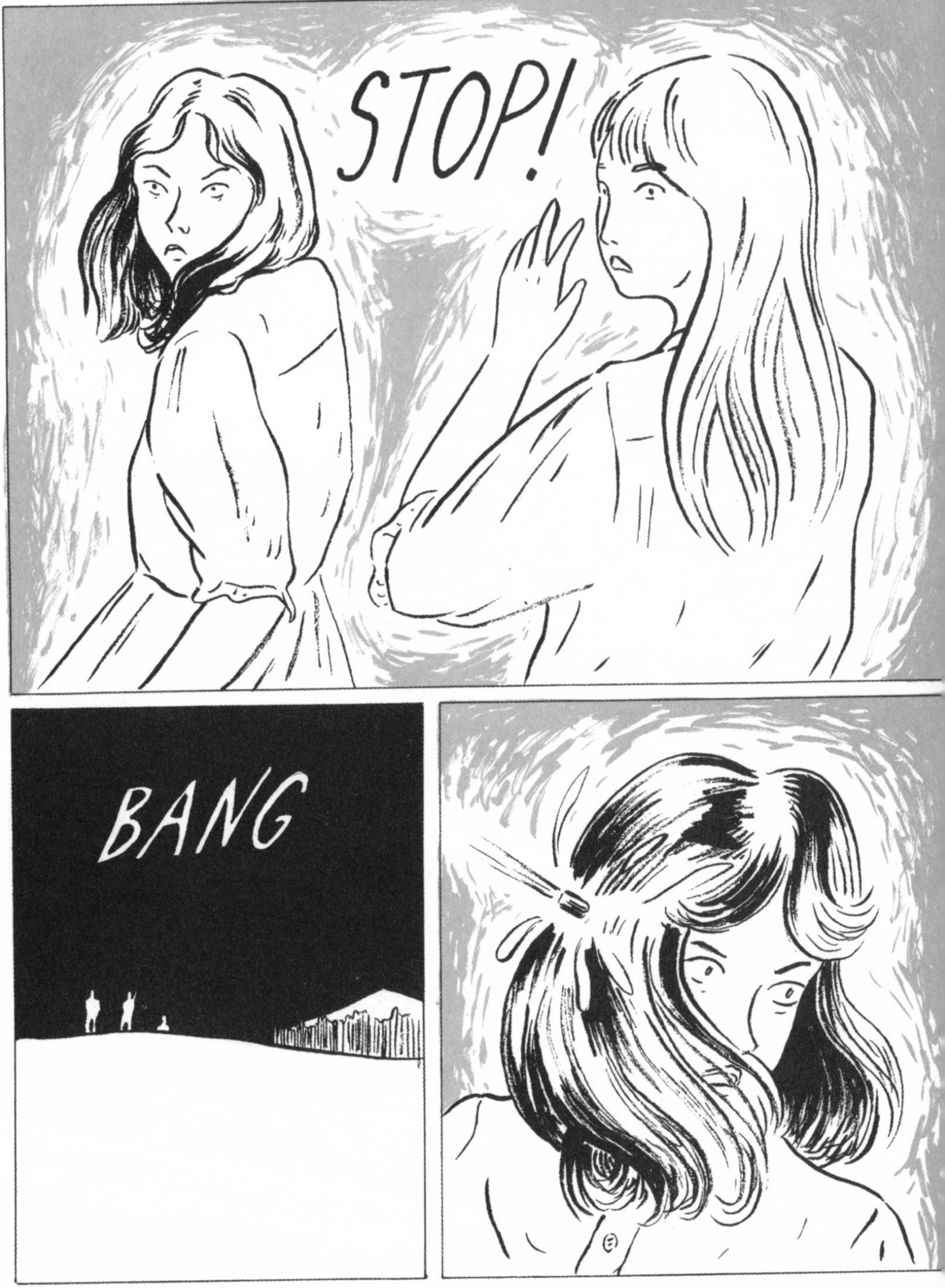
STOP!
BANG

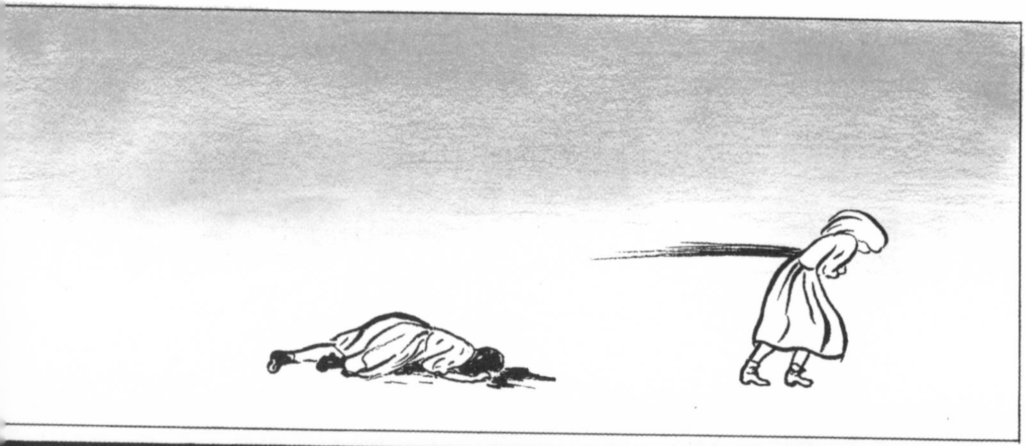

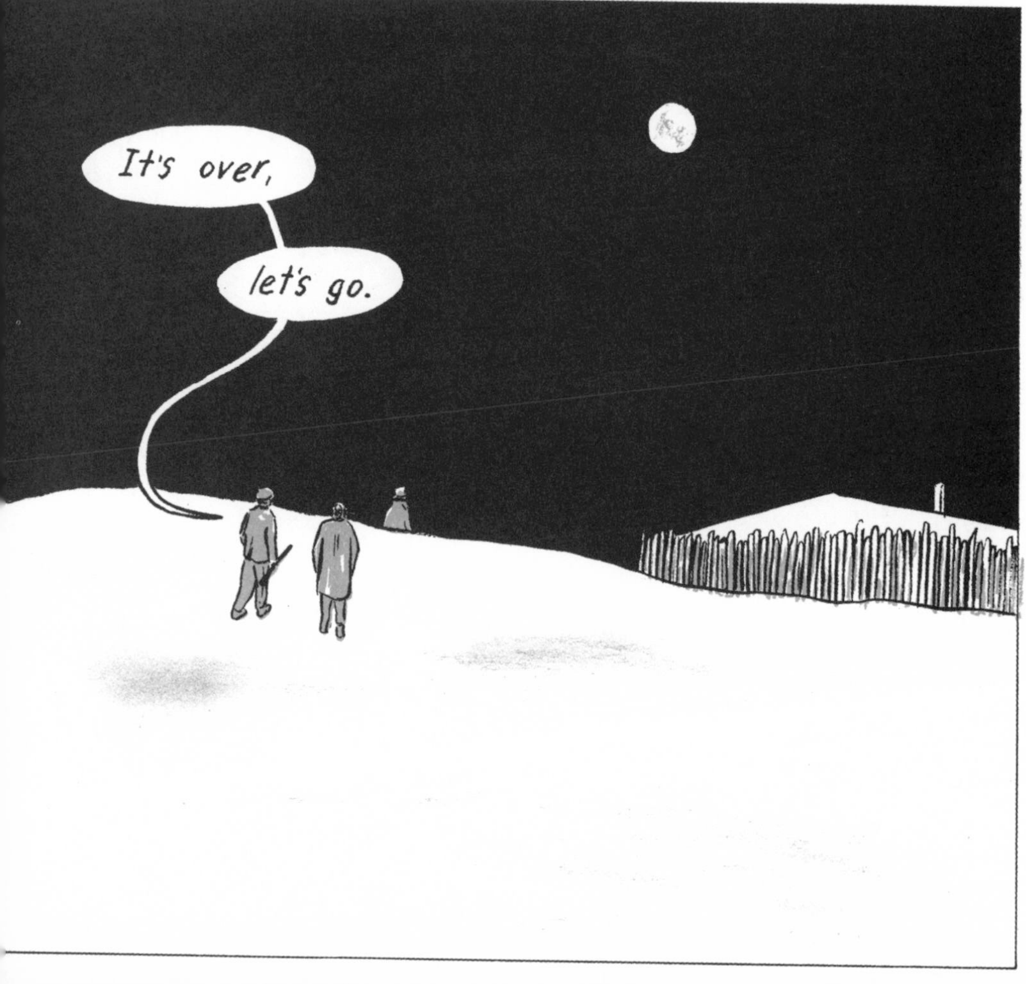
It's over,
let's go.

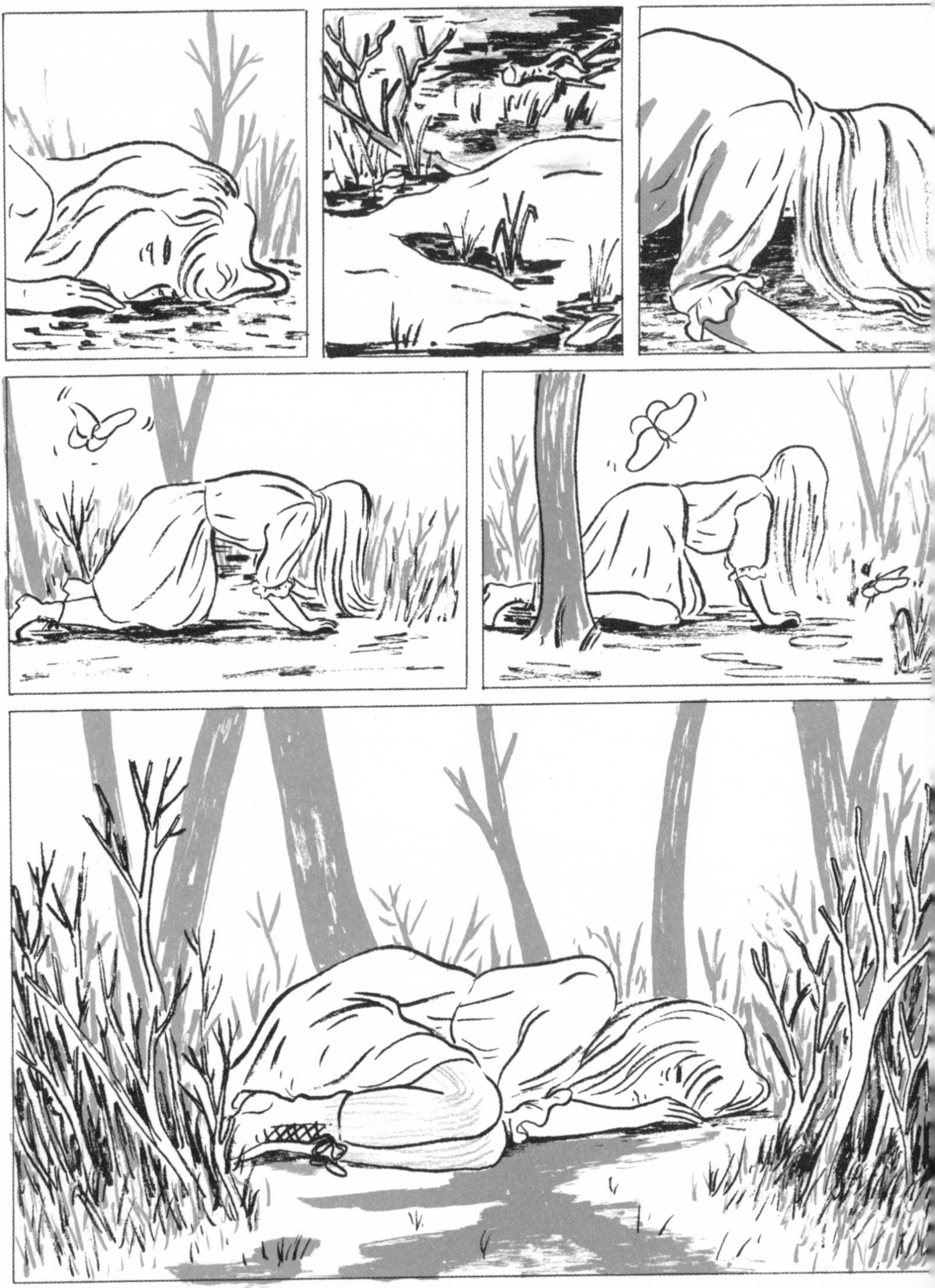

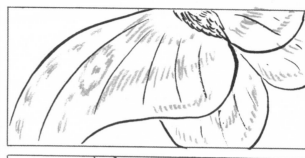

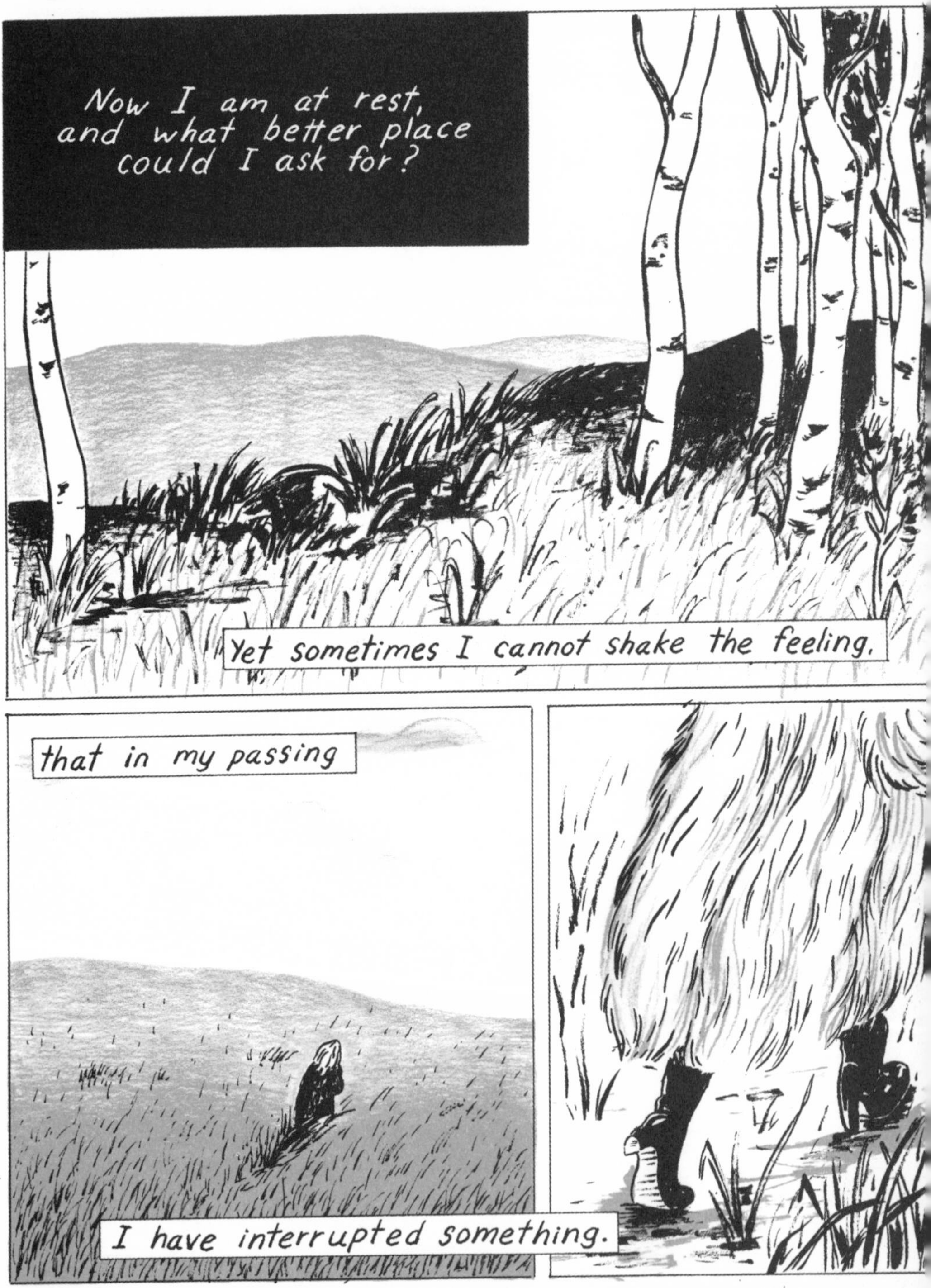
Now I am at rest, and what better place could I ask for?
Yet sometimes I cannot shake the feeling.
that in my passing
I have interrupted something.

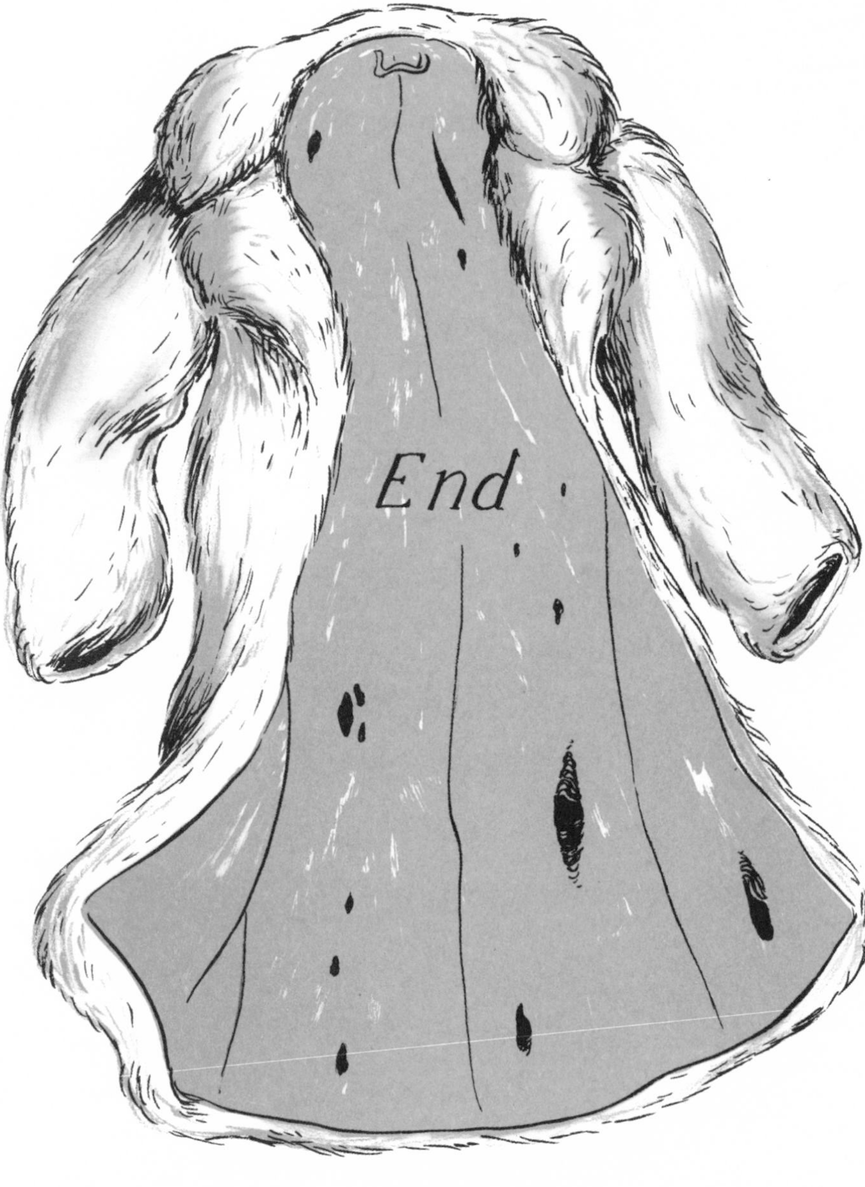
End

## Notes and Acknowledgements

In writing The Gift I have strayed from historical fact in many dates, settings and details. In both my research and inspiration for this book I am indebted to the many anonymous people who have spent their spare time making the Romanov family photographs and other documentation available online, as well as my teachers, classmates and friends who have given me feedback over the years.

Thank you to Paige, without whose love, enthusiasm and general brilliance I'm not sure this book would have come to fruition, to my Mum for unequivocally supporting everything I do, and my Nain, who makes me want to draw. Thank you to Andy and Sarah at Conundrum Press for everything, and thank you to Raph and Zinnia for the drawing emergency rescue.

Zoe Maeve is a comics artist originally from Tkaronto/Toronto who is now based in Tiohtià:ke/Montreal. She studied visual arts at Concordia University and in 2016 her book July Underwater was the recipient of Best English Comic at the Expozine Awards. She currently shares her home with one feisty black cat.